INTERNATIONAL NARRATIVES ON BECOMING A TEACHER EDUCATOR

INTERNATIONAL NARRATIVES ON BECOMING A TEACHER EDUCATOR

Pathways to a Profession

Edited by

George A. Churukian

and

Corey R. Lock

Mellen Studies in Education
Volume 42

The Edwin Mellen Press
Lewiston•Queenston•Lampeter

Library of Congress Cataloging-in-Publication Data

International narratives on becoming a teacher educator : pathways to
a profession / edited by George A. Churukian and Corey R. Lock.
   p. cm. -- (Mellen studies in education : v. 42)
   ISBN 0-7734-8015-3 (hard)
   1. Teacher educators Biography. 2. Teacher educators--Training
of. 3. Education--Study and teaching (Higher) I. Churukian,
George Allen, 1932- . II. Lock, Corey. III. Series.
LB1737.5.I58 1999
370'.71 ' 1--dc21   99-21897
                                                    CIP

This is volume 42 in the continuing series
Mellen Studies in Education
Volume 42 ISBN 0-7734-8015-3
MSE Series ISBN 0-88946-935-0

A CIP catalog record for this book is available from the British Library.
Cover Design Copyright © 1998 Martha E. Churukian

The Edwin Mellen Press   The Edwin Mellen Press
Box 450   Box 67
Lewiston, New York   Queenston, Ontario
USA 14092-0450   CANADA L0S 1L0

The Edwin Mellen Press, Ltd.
Lampeter, Ceredigion, Wales
UNITED KINGDOM SA48 8LT

Printed in the United States of America

This book is dedicated to our wives,
Carol and Grace, for their patience,
understanding, and encouragement.

Contents

NARRATIVES BY THE EDITORS

Foreword

I was feeling decidedly uncomfortable as my turn approached to present my paper at the 1998 International Society for Teacher Education's Seminar held in South Africa. I had written an account of mentoring international students at my University and such a personal narrative had been undertaken with reluctance and in a self-conscious vain. A colleague I confided in surprised me when she said that an autobiographical approach was highly regarded and indeed the latest research technique. I had never been accused of being on the frontier of educational research before so this news didn't make me feel any more at ease. I was quite amazed also when members of my paper group responded so enthusiastically to my paper and urged me to write more in this way. However, as this book shows, many of my ISTE friends and others were already busy writing their own personal stories. The wealth of their experiences and the tales they tell give evidence of the power of narrative. Not only are their stories interesting and revealing but they also illustrate the abiding commitment of teacher educators around the world to the value of education.

As I read I was first struck by the diversity of life experiences and the way in which each author chose to tell his or her story. Often I could hear the familiar voice of the storyteller in my mind's ear. The different accounts also show that teacher educators in all countries have very different opportunities in pursuing their own education and career paths. It seemed to me that being a male generally offered greater chances and fewer obstacles to a career than those faced by our women colleagues and, despite efforts to remedy this situation, I wonder how much things have really changed.

These stories also illustrate the great differences between learning and teaching in cities and remote country areas, between one teacher schools and large institutions, between pre-schools, elementary schools, high schools and universities, religious, private and state systems and those based on distinctive educational theories, philosophies, faiths and socio-economic systems. Ultimately I was faced with the only sensible answer to reconciling these differences: I had to strive to understand each account against the culture and environment of the story-teller and the society in which they live and work.

In making such an effort the reader will be rewarded not only by a good read but will discover some enlightening themes that run through most of the stories. It seems to me that the teacher educators who tell their stories here are imbued with a love for children which goes well beyond sentiment to a firm determination to play a significant part in each child's development. They are also people who enjoy helping learners of all ages. They hold knowledge in high regard and strive throughout their life to pursue learning through scholarship and research. They appreciate the power of language and communication and recognise the part this will play in the global village of the next millennium. Most have long experience of the hard world of daily work in the face of disappointments, frustrations and the burdens of office. Despite this they are resolute and serene.

I also rejoiced in finding more than a few authors who were determinedly subversive of received wisdom. They dared to ask questions even when such behaviour was discouraged or forbidden. Do I hear someone asking, "Who will rid me of this troublesome teacher?" Well I say, let us make him or her a teacher educator!

Throughout these stories we can see the wonderful way teacher educators have not only coped with change but have initiated, advocated, and encouraged it in the name of their charges--the teachers of tomorrow. As true professionals they could not do otherwise.

Join in the opportunity to celebrate the life and work of the teacher educators who tell their stories in this splendid book.

Warren Halloway
University of New England
Armidale, New South Wales,
Australia
December 1998

Acknowledgements

We wish to thank Warren Halloway, Secretary General of the International Society for Teacher Education (ISTE) for writing a commendatory preface to the book.

We are indebted to all the contributors to the volume who were willing to tell their "story" on becoming teacher educators. We thank them for the time and effort they put into writing and revising their respective narrative and their patience with us from the germination of the idea to this final product.

We acknowledge Carol Churukian's critiquing of each narrative, making many helpful suggestions.

We thank Martha Churukian for designing the cover of this publication.

We appreciate Jenny Hand's help with the word processing requirements needed to complete this manuscript.

George A. Churukian
Corey R. Lock

Introduction: Pathways To A Profession

George A. Churukian
Corey R. Lock

It is unlikely that many children announce their intentions to become teacher educators as they are growing up. Yet, colleges and universities through their teacher preparation programs find professors and others who have chosen to make a career of preparing teachers for the schools. Where does the journey to teacher education begin, and how varied is the road from country to country? We decided to ask a number of teacher educators from around the world to tell us the "story" of how they became teachers of teachers. The narratives included in this publication tell the stories of how twenty-four individuals, from twenty-four countries, became teacher educators.

We began this project by asking: How do people in countries around the world become teacher educators? Through our involvement with an association of world-wide teacher educators, we invited forty-three teacher educators from thirty-two countries to tell the story of how they became teacher educators. They were chosen to participate in the project by four criteria: their demonstrated knowledge of teacher education in their respective countries, their ability to use expressive language skills, their ability to express themselves in written English, and their geographic representation. The selection took into account gender and current professional position.

Each individual was sent a personal letter explaining the nature of the study and an invitation to become part of the project. Accompanying the letter was a detailed writing guide that described the areas the teacher educators were to include in their narratives. Specifically, each teacher educator was asked to incorporate the following information in his or her own "story."

- Tell something about who you are. (name, age, years in education)
- Tell where you work and explain your work. (who you teach, what are your students preparing to teach, what are you teaching them to know and do as teachers?)
- Tell what academic and non-academic activities your institution expects of you when you are not teaching. (may include research, public school involvement, or activities unique to your position)
- Tell what professional experiences you had as an educator that led to your current position as a teacher educator?
- Tell what preparation and expertise individuals in your position are expected to have in order to become a teacher educator. (college degrees, teaching experience, administrative background)
- Tell if there are changing requirements and/or expectations for how individuals become teacher educators. If so, in what ways?

The key instructions told the participants that the purpose of the project was to tell the "story" of how they became teacher educators and to describe the nature of their work. They were to keep in mind the question: "How can I, in an interesting manner, tell someone unfamiliar with teacher education, how an individual becomes a teacher educator?"

In the process of editing, we have attempted to keep the "voice" of each teacher educator. We have corrected any necessary grammatical errors and have smoothed out some the awkward word usage. In some cases we have kept the English spelling rather than the American spelling of various words. We have arranged the narratives in alphabetical order by country. Some of our colleagues were born and educated in one country but teach in another country. The country indicated under each teacher educator's name is the country in which she or he is teaching or taught.

We present to you, in the following pages, a series of vignettes written by our colleagues on how they became teacher educators. As you read these personal "stories," we hope you will have a sense of what each person had to do to become a teacher educator and learn the nature of that person's work from his or her culture. In theses vignettes you may find evidence closely paralleling your life or the life of other teacher educators you may know.

2

Each "story" is unique, yet there is a thread of similarity that runs through each. Even though teacher educators from different parts of the world have different languages and cultures, we all share similar paths and can relate our own experiences to those which are presented here. We all share the same frustrations with colleagues from other disciplines, with administration, and with education ministries. Yet, we all share the love and desire to help others learn so that they may become better individuals in our respective societies.

Teacher Education: To Meet Educational Challenges

Wendy Crebbin
Australia

I have been a teacher educator since 1981, most of that time as a part-time tutor, and later a lecturer, at the University of Ballarat. During that same time, I continued to teach in secondary schools for a couple of years; did continuous part-time study for 12 years; worked four years in a second part-time tutoring position, at Deakin University, Geelong; gained two government grants to enhance university teaching; and, mostly as a single parent, raised one family, and began another. I finally attained the status of being full-time, and a senior lecturer, in 1996.

During 1996 - 1998 I was on leave from the University of Ballarat and worked on a two year contract as an Advisor for Teacher Education with the SIDA (Swedish) funded Teacher Education Reform Program (TERP), at the National Institute for Educational Development in Namibia.

The pathway between my early experiences and expectations, and my current position as a teacher educator and an advisor, seems to be full of happen-stance, rather than any pre-defined plan.

I was born in 1942 in a small rural community and grew up on a farm where practical knowledge and the flow of the seasons were more important than schooling. My movement into teaching initially came more directly through my desire for economic independence and the subsequent gaining of a teaching studentship which paid my university fees and provided a small living allowance, rather than any great desire to be a teacher. In this, I was fortunate that the late 1950's and early 1960's was a time of rapid growth in secondary education in Victoria with a consequent intense shortage of teachers.

My first degree was a two year Diploma of Physical Education at Melbourne University, and a further year at Secondary Teachers' College, which qualified me to teach English and geography as well as physical education. I taught in government secondary schools from 1962 to 1969. For most secondary teachers in those years their working environment was in new schools, with very inadequate facilities. For me, in one case, when I began at the school there was not even a school building. Even at that early stage of my career I have vivid memories of running into problems with the 'authorities' because I could see that what we were teaching was not related to the lives and needs of the students.

In 1969 I had to resign from teaching because of the imminent birth of my first child and because there was no provision for maternity leave at that time.

When I wanted to resume my teaching career in 1977, after having three children, working as a journalist, and running a country newspaper for a few years, I was informed that teacher registration requirements had changed and I needed an extra year of training. So, whilst maintaining my work on the newspaper, I returned to full-time study at Ballarat College of Advanced Education (BCAE), which was situated about 80 km from my home. The course I enrolled in was a three year Diploma of General Studies (Dip. G.S.). This was later converted to a B.A. degree which I completed with majors in Psychology and Sociology. In 1978 I sold the newspaper and moved with my children to Ballarat, to concentrate on my studies. Ballarat is a rural city in Victoria, with a population of about 80,000. Education is one of the main industries in the city, with two universities and many private schools as well as state primary and secondary schools.

In my Dip. G.S., and later in the B.A., I was able to negotiate independent research studies, working with non-readers in a nearby secondary school. With the support of one of the physical education teachers and a 'remedial teacher' in the school, I devised, implemented, and evaluated a program based on a theory of improving learning through perceptual motor activities. Through this process I became very conscious of the complexity of learning, and the large number of students who had great difficulty, or who do not fit the 'norms' of our education system.

On completion of my studies I became re-registered as a secondary teacher, but because of economic circumstances, no new teachers were being employed. So I resumed my teaching career in 1980 as an emergency teacher, filling in for absent teachers and frequently getting calls at 8:15 a.m. to begin teaching at 8:45.

As an alternative to this, I applied for and obtained two consecutive 16 week contracts as a remedial teacher in a program called Education for Unemployed Youth (EPUY) which was funded by the Australian Federal Government for people between the ages of 16 and 23.

These programs were supposed to be for students who had basic literacy and numerical skills. What we soon found was that many of the young people were unemployed because their skills were so minimal that they could not read employment vacancy signs or fill in application forms. We also found that quite a number of them had been in trouble with the police because of 'anti-social behaviour' ranging from vandalism to theft and violence. What I learned from this work was how badly our schooling system serves some of our quite able, 'normal', young people who, for a variety of reasons, have not learned well in school. I also learned that many different groups are rightly suspicious about the value of schooling in their lives. Importantly, from these students, I also learned what it means for young people when they feel that they have been defined as inadequate.

Nearing the end of my second contract, and not wanting to be unemployed myself, I applied for a part-time tutoring position in educational psychology at BCAE. I was surprised and elated when I was offered a few hours tutoring a week. For the first two years, before I received enough tutoring hours to work almost full time, I supplemented my income by continuing emergency teaching two or three days a week in three local secondary schools.

In this inauspicious way my work in teacher education began. However my reasons for staying in teacher education are quite deliberate and intentional. After so many experiences which strengthened my understandings of the ways in which education was, and is, not serving the needs of students, I determined to work towards trying to better equip the next generation of teachers to deal with these issues.

Over the next few years I gradually increased the areas in which I tutored, moving into teaching Classroom Processes, and taking classes in primary, secondary, and physical education teacher education courses. I also took on more and more

7

responsibility for planning organising and administering the courses. Gradually my employment pattern changed too. My work was defined as 'fractional' rather than 'associate staff,' and at the end of 1988 I was granted a tenured 0.7 position.

As my employment pattern changed towards developing a career in teacher education, my Head of School advised me that I needed to improve my qualifications. So in 1985, wanting to enter a master's program, and again being told that my qualifications were not appropriate because my B.Aa came after my teaching qualifications, rather than before, I enrolled as a part-time, off-campus student in a Graduate Diploma of Educational Administration at Deakin University, Geelong. I completed the program in three years whilst working almost full time and also having another child. In the next four years (1988-91), I completed my Master of Educational Administration degree. I then enrolled in Ph.D. studies and worked diligently, to the point of being close to completion, before taking a break because of other demands and changing directions in my life.

These changes, as with so many of the other significant impacts in my life, seem to have developed as a result of what appeared at the time to be small events rather than as cross-roads. In this instance the changes are also closely connected to changes and new expectations as well as initiatives, challenges and opportunities within higher education in Australia.

Ballarat University is one of the newest and smallest of the Universities in Australia, but as an educational institution it has a history which dates back over 100 years. Ballarat became a university in 1994 through a series of national Government initiatives which, by amalgamations, established 36 large universities rather than maintaining over 100 smaller institutions. At the same time they ended the former binary system where Universities had almost all of the research and post-graduate teaching as well as undergraduates, whilst Colleges of Advanced Education (CAEs) were almost entirely directed towards undergraduate education.

The history of the University of Ballarat in some ways is similar to many former Teacher Education Colleges and Colleges of Advanced Education throughout Australia. It was established in 1976 through the amalgamation of the Ballarat Institute of Advanced Education (formerly part of The School of Mines and Industries, Ballarat) and the State College of Victoria at Ballarat (formerly Ballarat Teachers College). As a result of this amalgamation, BCAE offered courses in mining and engineering, applied science, business studies, humanities, librarianship, and education. Since the amalgamation nursing, psychology, and creative arts have been added.

The School of Education, like many similar faculties, has been greatly reduced in recent years and now has less than 20 full-time academic staff who, with the assistance of an increasing number of graduate student tutors, are responsible for teaching some 400 full time undergraduate students and more than 300, mostly part time, graduate students. The courses include a four year B.A./B.T. each which qualifies students to teach in primary schools; one year Graduate Diploma of Education for secondary teachers; the education component of the four year Post-Primary Physical Education Degree; plus a rapidly growing graduate studies area which includes Graduate Diplomas in Computing, Education Administration, Vocational Education, Teaching in High Education, Master of Education by coursework or research, and some Ph.D. students.

The expertise required for a teacher educator has changed over the years. This has been influenced by the changing circumstances and expectations of education, at all levels. So that, whilst experience as a teacher continues to be a prerequisite for employment in teacher education in Australia, it would be very unlikely now for anyone to be employed, even as a tutor, without some graduate qualification, or at least some part of a master degree.

The normal teaching load in the University of Ballarat is about sixteen hours per week, or approximately 45% of our time. Besides this, teacher education lecturers are responsible for the organisation of the units including working with colleagues and tutors, planning and writing course materials, monitoring students' progress, supervising student teachers in their school placements, and being available for students who need extra assistance. There is no defined proportion of our time allocated for these latter tasks. They, like research, consultancy work, administrative tasks, and meetings, are a part of the day-to-day work.

With the change in status to a university, there is a greater expectation that we will be involved in research, publication, and applying for research grants. Because of the increasing demands on time, as well as the applied nature of my teaching and research interests, I have found that I need to use the time when I am out in schools working with student teachers, or providing professional development for teachers, to also collect material for my research. Most of my writing is done at home very early in the mornings or at weekends.

Another change in expectations, deliberately introduced by the Australian national government in the early 1990's, was an emphasis on improving the quality of teaching in universities. To promote this emphasis the government provided funds for competitive grants. In 1992, as a result of a very small internal allocation which allowed me to work with the Engineering Faculty at BU, I gained an insight into teaching and courses in another faculty. And, with this knowledge, I led a team in a successful application to gain funds to introduce and enhance notions of teaching and learning through collaborative problemsolving with academics and first year students in Business, Nursing, Engineering, Education, Applied Science, and Computing.

In the following year this work, which I did in addition to my work as a teacher educator, continued with the support of additional monies from the university. In 1994 & 1995 I continued the development work with academics, support staff, and students, with a second national grant, working with another team to enhance the teaching, learning, and communication of complex knowledges with the aid of concept mapping and computer texts, across all sections of the university. All of which has meant that I have been able to apply my knowledge of teaching and learning not only in teacher education, but with academics and students across the whole institution.

In teacher education the major focus of my teaching in recent years has been to enable students to become aware of the complexity of the processes of learning and to be willing and able to look at the learning of their students, and question and examine assumed connections between teaching, learning, and assessment. Thus, I try to support the development of student teachers so they will become knowledgeable about public theories of teaching/learning and the implications of those theories in practice, and also that they will become good practitioners, able to critique their own, and other's ideas in the light of the needs of their students.

In 1996 my interest in recognising the complexity of learning and attempting to enhance teaching led my Head of School and university to nominate me for an opportunity to seek out alternative interpretations, in a different setting. The success of this nomination meant that, I was able to spend the latter half of that year working and learning in England and Europe.

It was during this time that happenstance intervened again. I learnt about, and applied for, the position which I held in Namibia. My role was to provide guidance, advice and support for Namibians at NIED, and in the four teacher education

10

colleges, in their development of the new national teacher education program. The government policy documents define teacher education as leading the reform of education in this country to meet the goals of democracy, access, equity, and quality. Key ideals which relate those goals to teaching and learning in Namibia are the importance of individual and cultural diversity; personal and social respect and responsibility; and gaining knowledge through challenging and meaningful experiences. These ideals are believed to be best attained through the use of learner-centred and positive approaches and through teachers taking a critical, analytical, reflective and creative approach to their teaching.

Whilst my term here was limited to two years, I believe that the experience enabled me to learn a great deal about education in this new and developing country, as well as to apply what I have learned through other experiences, and again to test, reflect on, and evaluate my own values and beliefs about teaching and learning.

Unlike Namibia, in Australia in the past, teachers have not been encouraged to take a strong interest in the politics of education, or to see their role as a political one. Therefore, they have remained outside of the processes whereby particular discourses about the purposes and value of education, as well as fairly simplistic propositions about teaching and learning, have become dominant, whilst others have been subsumed or pushed aside. One consequence of this in recent years, is that ideas which connect teaching and learning with views of the person as a personal relationship have been marginalised, whilst economic meanings of education have become more powerful.

In my view the most serious problem which confronts education in Australia, and possibly other parts of the world, is a lack of recognition of the politics, values, and assumptions about education which shape the complex demands which are placed on teachers and learners today. There have been continued pressures for more and varied kinds of knowledges to be inserted into the already crowded curriculum and, at the same time, continued cuts in the budgets for public education. The increasing demands placed on education, and on students, have meant that students are expected to stay at school longer and to graduate with an increasing array of competencies which will make them more adaptable in the diminishing employment markets. Which means that, at a time of decreasing funding for public schooling, there are more students in the school system with less facilities, and less teachers. These expectations are being made more difficult for teachers to deal with because

11

many of the problems of learning and learners which I encountered with 'low-achieving students' before I began working in teacher education are still not being addressed. There are some very good programs in Australian primary schools for identifying non-readers, but there are still children who slip through the net. And, at the top end of secondary school, the problem is being made worse because young people who have defined themselves as failures at school, and who want to leave, have little option except to stay on and get more-of-the-same.

All of this means that people who have become teachers because they care for young people and want them to have opportunities to learn, to grow and develop, are finding that they are becoming increasingly frustrated and disillusioned. Yet these are the very people whom I believe are needed within the education system.

To make future teachers better able to cope with the differences between their desires and the reality, and between the rhetoric and the economically driven choices which governments are making, I believe that teacher education needs to provide teachers with a political understanding of the discourses which surround education.

What I am advocating is not that all teachers should be overtly political, but that, in addition to having practical knowledge and experiences, student teachers need to be equipped to understand and contest propositions about education which go against what they know about good teaching and learning. This means that teacher education should include the values which underpin different ideas about teaching and learning, and an acknowledgement of the importance of teachers and learners as people with their own needs, interests, and cultural backgrounds

My Teacher Education Story

Zoya Kolontai
Belarus

Of all the professions I know of, the profession of teacher, in my opinion, is the most unique. It touches the souls of students, and requires special people with a full understanding of their responsibility and mission and the trust which other people place on them. As we give ourselves and the selves of people most dear to us into the hands of teachers, we would like these hands to be the hands of masters and not of apprentices.

What makes a good teacher? Why did I decide to become a teacher and a teacher educator? Why through all of my career have I constantly come back to education? These are not the easiest questions I have been asking myself throughout my life.

I was born in 1952 in Minsk, Belarus. My educational background includes ten years at a secondary school specialized in the English language in Minsk. Then I studied for five years at Minsk State Pedagogical Institute of Foreign Languages (now the Linguistic University) and later at the post-graduate school of the same Institute. My dissertation paper was on vocational education in Great Britain, and it was among the first in its field in the former Soviet Union. Upon defending it I was awarded the degree of Candidate Of Sciences (Education).

I started my work at Minsk State Pedagogical Institute of Foreign Languages in 1975, the year I graduated from it. It was not a very widespread practice to admit people immediately after graduation, but at that time there was a need for instructors

13

in the Italian language, which was my second specialty. Besides, I had the required diploma with honors degree and experience working as an interpreter. Participation in the research during my student years was also taken into consideration.

In Belarus to be admitted as a teacher educator to the pedagogical institute or university one should meet the following requirements: pedagogical and research qualification (academic degree and status), type of specialty, length of service and experience, and compliance with the interests of the division.

All academic positions in pedagogical and other institutes are filled on a competitive basis. Every five years a teacher educator has to be re-elected, and the vacancy is advertised. To pass the competition and be elected for the next five-year period to the same or a higher position, a teacher educator has to demonstrate improvement in her/his skills and qualifications (for example, to defend a dissertation and be awarded an academic degree, to take some special inservice courses or to carry out research). Lately, more attention is being paid to the personal qualities of faculty members and their ability to work with the audience, to "hear" every student in the academic group. Thus, now a teacher educator without an academic degree but experienced and successful in her/his long teaching service may be elected to the position of the assistant professor, which was unprecedented only a few years ago.

So, for a number of years I worked as an instructor in the English language of the fourth and fifth year students at the Department of the English Language of Minsk State Pedagogical Institute of Foreign Languages. I conducted seminars and practical studies, as well assisted during the exams.

Later, my interest in research in education and in teaching brought me to the Division of Education and to the post-graduate school. Working at the Division of Education, I taught theory and history of education to the third year students and supervised the fourth year students in their practice at school. We worked in close contact with teachers and administrators of schools where our students were student teaching. We conducted planning and instructional meetings with the school teachers before the practice, carried out joint intermediate control, and assessed the results and students' achievements at the end of the practice.

I was fortunate in being able to work with many interesting and experienced faculty who were committed to the profession of teaching and

14

devoted to students. Working side by side with such people one cannot but follow their example. Looking back, I realize how important it is for beginning teachers to have mentors who are eager to advise and to assist. I believe this is one of the most important elements in professional development of educators.

My teacher education background and experience was very beneficial in my duties later, when in 1986 I was elected the district council deputy-chairperson in one of the districts of Minsk. Among the areas of my responsibility at that time were education and child-care from the pre-kindergarten to the university levels. Similarly, I feel that my years of work at the district council, and later at the Research Institute of Pedagogical Education and as a Secretary General of the National Commission of Belarus for UNESCO have contributed much to my development as a teacher educator and enriched me with valuable knowledge and experience, which I can share with my students now.

The district of Minsk, where I worked, was like a town in a big city. It is one of the nine districts into which Minsk is administratively divided and it has the population of about 200,000 people. At the time when I worked as a deputy-mayor there were twenty-one schools, a dozen kindergartens, two vocational-technical schools and one higher education institute. A great part of my time was spent in these educational establishments, especially in schools. I had to see that all conditions necessary for running schools were provided. I had also to coordinate activities of different district council's departments in relation to education.

All these gave me good insight into the school life besides the educational process itself. It also helped me to better understand the interrelation between different educational institutions, and the continuous character of education. I got a better vision of the role and place of a school in the life of the community and the society in general. As time went on, the feeling that I should share this knowledge and attitude with future teachers and thus contribute to their professional preparation began to come to me more and more often.

It was in 1990 that a new research institute of pedagogical education was organized in Minsk as part of the U.S.S.R. Academy of Pedagogical Sciences. I was proposed to head the department which concentrated on research in the field of best foreign and domestic practices in teacher education. I had to make my choice and I made it in favor of this institute. The possibility to research teacher education in different parts of the Soviet Union and abroad and thus to help practicing teacher educators in their endeavors to improve educational system sounded to me attractive and promising.

All of us, who came to work at the institute, were very enthusiastic and full of hope. Several projects in different areas of teacher preparation were started. The department I chaired began to work on a project in comparative teacher education covering different countries of the world. I feel deep sorrow when I think that the institute existed only slightly more than one year. One of the results of the disintegration of the Soviet Union was that many all-Union institutions located in the former republics and financed by the central government didn't have the source of finance any more and ceased to exist. Many researchers went to work as educators to the teacher education institutes and universities. I got the proposal to work at the Ministry of Foreign Affairs of Belarus, where in 1992-1993 I had the position of the Secretary General of the National Commission of Belarus for UNESCO (United Nations Educational, Scientific and Cultural Organization).

In 1993 I received a Fulbright Scholarship and left for the U.S.A. where I did research on teacher education in different countries. It was a continuation and further development of the project that I started at the Research Institute of Pedagogical Education in 1990. On my return home, I organized the Education Advisory Center in Minsk, of which I became the director. One of the aims of this center is to assist students, teachers and teacher educators, who would like to learn more about education in general, and teacher education in particular, in different countries. The center is not an alternative form of teacher education. We would like to help those, who teach or learn how to teach, to get additional knowledge and information, which will help them in their professional development.

The educational programs in teacher training institutes in Belarus usually consist of three blocks of subjects: a block of the disciplines of future specialty, a block of pedagogical and psychological disciplines, and a block of social sciences and general subjects. Instruction in pedagogy goes alongside training in other disciplines and is allocated to different years of study.

Tradition that dates back to 1930s did not allow teacher educators to diverge from a centrally devised curriculum, and the content of education was practically the same in all teacher education institutions throughout the Soviet Union. Later regional components were introduced to the curricula which brought teacher education

16

institutions closer to the needs of the regions of institutes' locations. In the 1990s teacher education institutions received the right to develop their own course programs and curricula, which should be in conformity with state requirements and goals.

Thus it has become much more interesting and challenging to work as a teacher educator today than it was in 1975 when I began my teaching career.

As a matter of fact, when, as a 17-year old girl, I entered the institute, becoming a teacher was not my primary goal. My first love was the English language, the language of Shakespeare and Galsworthy, of London and Hemingway. I wanted to be able to read, to travel, to learn more about other countries and places. The knowledge of foreign languages could help me to do that. I wanted to better understand people who lived in other parts of the world. They seemed to me to be very different and at the same time so much like us, the people who lived in the U.S.S.R. The pedagogical institute of foreign languages was at that time the only place where a girl could prepare herself for that vocation.

Love for teaching came later. Or, it might have always been somewhere deep inside me, so that the favorable conditions of a teacher education institution helped it to come to the surface and flower.

Among these conditions, the model of teacher educators is undoubtedly one of the most important. The level of knowledge of the faculty, the methods of instruction they use, their manner of treatment of students, and moral and civic image are the factors of great potential power for future teachers. The personal and professional development of students should be carried out through the individual influence of scholars who work with them.

In my life such scholars were Dr. Tamara Kharitonova, the supervisor of my diploma project, and Professor Yuri Kovalenko, the supervisor of my post-graduate studies. They helped a lot in my development as a teacher educator, a researcher, and as an individual. They, like many other educators, acted on the premises that a student was an active subject of the education. For them to educate and teach meant not only to give knowledge to an individual, but rather to teach to learn, and to help students develop their abilities, skills, and creative potential.

This mission of teacher educators was not shared by everyone at that time. For many years the prevailing attitude toward students and school pupils was as objects rather than subjects of the educational process. The active role was believed to belong to the educators. Changes in the economic and social situation in Belarus, caused by the proclamation of its sovereignty in 1990 and the disintegration of the Soviet Union, the transition to a market economy, and national rebirth led to the change in educational policy and practice.

Teaching and educational process in pedagogical institutes is being reorganized in such a way that it develops independent creative thinking, cognitive approach, broad world outlook, general and professional culture, national self-consciousness in future teachers. It is understood that only teachers with such qualities will be able to carry out the new task that society had set up for them -to mold in students social qualities of a person who will be a part of the society, based on market economy relations.

This task is of a revolutionary character, because it presupposes fundamental changes in philosophy, content, and methodological approaches to the education of teachers. It also means that teacher educators have to determine themselves their place in the new system, and what ideals and goals they will orient their students towards. For many of us, this means that we have to make our choices, review former values, and understand and adjust to the new economic, social, and political situation in the country. For me as for many people who were born, educated and brought up in the Soviet Union, this process was painstaking and very often stressful.

The challenges teacher educators have to face nowadays are multiform. The attempts undertaken to answer these challenges are diverse. The role and functions of educators, as well as qualifications they are required to have, are undergoing changes. But whatever comes, I have a strong belief that to be a teacher educator it takes a lot more than merely to have pedagogical experience of working at school or other educational institution and to know well one's subject matter. One should also know different sides of life in order to educate future teachers and to help them to prepare themselves to the great mission of a leader.

My Circuitous Way to Becoming a Teacher Educator

Michael Bamidele Adeyemi
Botswana

The idea of becoming a teacher educator came to me when I was attending elementary school in Nigeria. I was about 10 years old in the year 1960, when Nigeria became independent. Why and how I thought about the idea were beyond my imagination. I guessed there were no professional options at that time. Perhaps the "elites" of the society at that time were mainly teachers and catechists. The elementary school in question was All Saints' Primary School, Osogbo, Nigeria. Teacher candidates from the Primary College, the Provincial Grade II Teachers Training College were assigned to elementary schools on teaching practice annually as part of their professional development.

These teacher candidates were a source of inspiration to me in the sense that I assumed that after their training, they would assume high status in the society, perhaps next in hierarchy to the traditional ruler, the bishop and the school headmaster. Medical doctors, engineers, top civil servants were rare "commodities" at this time, and so thinking of becoming one of them did not cross my mind. My only option, particularly with respect to the high regard accorded a teacher was teaching as a profession.

I attended Osogbo Grammar School for my secondary education between 1963 and 1967, passing the West African School Certificate Examinations in Division One in 1967. Thereafter, I did the Higher School Certificate course at Oduduwa College, Ile-Ife between 1968 and 1969 and then gained an admission to read geography at the University of Ibadan between 1970 and 1973. My B.Sc. degree in geography was earned from the Faculty of Science since my minors were biology and geology. I had no formal training in teacher education.

In 1973, the Government established the Compulsory National Youth Service Corps whereby University graduates were assigned to work in areas beyond their immediate environment. This idea was to heal the wounds of the Nigerian Civil War of 1967-1970 and also to strengthen unity in an ethnically and multi-culturally diverse nation. I was assigned to teach geography in an elitist primary school, the Kaduna Capital School in then North Central State of Nigeria. Teaching here was not challenging to me because of the elementary nature of the syllabus and the pupils.

After my National Youth Service, I took up a teaching appointment at St. John's Catholic Grammar School, Ile-Ife, Nigeria. This was the first time I faced the challenges of a teacher. I taught biology and geography at this school between 1974 and 1977. First and foremost, I really enjoyed teaching my students. Many of them have become medical doctors, Ph.D. holders in their respective disciplines, editors of newspapers, lawyers and the like today. It was at this school that I was faced with a very big challenge which was to shape my life as a professional educator. This was the realization that there was a big gap between teachers with and without professional training.

I had no formal training in teacher education. Although, the knowledge of the subject matter was "there," I lacked the "methodology." No wonder then that I got exhausted quickly before the end of the day. Had I "armed" myself with the relevant training, I would have known how to better organize teaching sessions that would not easily snuff life out of me before the school closed each day. I then realized I needed to go back to school to be trained in teacher education.

This opportunity came in 1977 when I was appointed a teacher at Adeyemi College of Education (University of Ife), Ondo Campus. I enrolled at the University of Ife Main campus in the Faculty of Education to read for a master's degree in education (Curriculum Studies) with an emphasis on social studies education. This was completed in 1979. When a College of Education was established at Ilesa in the then Oyo State, I joined the teaching staff in 1979 to teach geography and social studies. I was the Head of the Department of Geography and Social Studies until 1982 when I gained admission as a graduate student in social studies education at Indiana University, Bloomington, Indiana, U.S.A. I obtained the M.S. and Ph.D.

degrees in social studies education in 1983 and 1985 respectively. I was a graduate assistant between 1983 and 1985 involved in the development of curriculum materials at the Social Studies Development Center at Indiana University, in addition to being a project staff member on "Internationalizing Teacher Education Program."

I returned to Nigeria in 1985 as a lecturer in social studies education at the University of Ife, now Obafemi Awolowo University. There I designed and taught social studies and supervised students in the new Bachelor of Education program. I also participated in the supervision of dissertations of post graduate students. Between 1991 and 1992, I was on sabbatical leave at the Department of Languages and Social Sciences Education, University of Botswana. I had the opportunity to infuse and teach social studies to Post Graduate Diploma in Education students. I returned to Obafemi Awolowo University in Nigeria in 1992. In 1994 I accepted a position at the University of Botswana, where I am currently a faculty member, first as a senior research fellow at the National Institute of Development Research and Documentation of the University, later as a senior lecturer, and now as an associate professor of social studies education in the Department of Languages and Social Sciences Education. I have brought to the University of Botswana a wealth of experience in social studies education. I have reviewed the undergraduate and postgraduate social studies programs, and educating future social studies educators in the country. The social studies undergraduates, upon graduation, are expected to teach at the Junior Secondary School level while those with master's degrees mainly teach at the colleges of education. The University of Botswana has about 8000 students. I have organized many workshops on social studies teaching, in addition to being the moderator of social studies in affiliated colleges in Botswana.

Teaching, research and publications, and service are the main criteria used in the review of academic staff for appointment, promotion, and renewal of contract. Teaching is made interesting at the university in that there are teaching facilities at ones disposal. The university library stocks thousands of social studies texts and access to the internet is easy. Almost all teachers have computers in their offices.

The University encourages the art of research and publication. Many journals are available in the library. The Higher Education Development Unit (HEDU), the School of Graduate Studies, the Botswana Educational Research Association (housed at the university), and many departments organize workshops on various issues including "How to Publish" at various fora.

I participate in many committees, both at the departmental and the faculty levels, in addition to providing my professional service to the community, for instance, organizing social studies workshops at various education centers in the country. There is no regulation governing the time allocated to teaching, research and service. However, I spend about 50% of my time on teaching and assessing students, 30% on research and 20% on service.

There is no educational system that is 100% perfect. Some shortcomings, particularly at the secondary school level are:

(1) The automatic promotion of primary school children into junior secondary schools. This has made effective teaching difficult because slow learners cannot learn at the same pace with the fast learners in the classroom. Perhaps, streamlining of students based on their abilities may solve the problem.

(2) Large class size of between 40-37 students in the classroom may make individual attention very difficult. Reduction in class size means provision of more teachers and classrooms on the part of government.

The government is trying hard to improve the standard of teacher education in Botswana. For instance, Primary Teacher Training Colleges have been upgraded to Colleges of Education. This implies that teachers at the Primary Schools will now be better qualified and better equipped to perform their professional duties.

While the above problems can be regarded as institutional, the traditional aspect of discipline which should be home based needs some thought. In many African countries, discipline of children is a major problem which can make or mar the successful development of the whole child. The enhancement of moral and intellectual development of the child can only be enhanced in the school setting if parents instill discipline at home. This is a challenge not only for Botswana, but for the universe as a whole. Our teacher education program should emphasize the production of responsible citizens who can contribute to the overall development of the nation and the world at large.

From Preacher's Kid to Professor:
The Story of an Educator

Nestor Luiz João Beck
Brazil

As I begin telling you this story of how I became an educator, please let me explain that I work part-time as a professor of educational philosophy in a graduate program at a Catholic university and full-time as a vice-president for graduate studies, research, and extension in a Lutheran university. In the master's and doctorate program in education I teach students who are teachers in elementary and high schools, or professors at universities and colleges maintained by the State, churches, and other community or private organizations. They are mostly women. Their pay is low, if compared to that of other professionals with equivalent training. Those who support a family with their earnings as teachers, usually work in several schools for as many as 60 hours a week.

This means that the teacher students I teach must struggle to survive. They want to become better teachers by understanding what they are doing and in finding ways of doing it even better. They do not have much time, however, to study and think. They are interested in theory only if it explains or improves their practice. They need help, concrete scientific help to pursue daily teaching. They expect me to provide such help. This expectation both frightens and excites me.

Perspective

In order to explain how I got into teaching, I must tell you the story of my life. As I look back on its course I see relations between the teaching I do now and the process by which I have become the person I regard myself as being. I realize that the perception I have of myself at this moment of life's trajectory may not be comprehensive. I am trying to be true, but I know that we all tend to tell pleasant stories about ourselves, and may end up deceiving ourselves and others on account of needs we are not aware of.

This life of mine, I understand, is the result of a complex interaction between myself and the persons who brought me up, and the circumstances which I have faced. As I regard the process whereby I am becoming who I am and am doing what I do, I realize that I am looking at the past from my present position in this moment's situation. If I were looking at the past from another position in another moment, my perception and understanding would be different, and I would be telling you a different story. Therefore, I believe, we will understand this story better if I tell you first where I stand or rather where I am sitting right now.

Please try to imagine me in my home study this Sunday morning: a fair-skinned, blue-eyed male, fifty-six years old. I am writing on a notebook. There are books all around me. They constitute my immediate world--along with family, the house, and the garden. In front of me, three shelves on education and philosophy in Portuguese, German, English, and (a few) in French: Paulo Freire, Habermas, Gadamer, Ricoeur, Max Weber, Marx, Dilthey, Locke, Pestalozzi, Rousseau, Comenius, Saint Augustine, Plato. Behind me, five wall-to-wall shelves on theology, mainly on the Bible and Luther, mostly in English and German. There are also German journals which have shaped my thinking: *Universitas and Lutherische Monatshefte*. On the wall, diplomas for undergraduate degrees in theology and philosophy and master's and doctor's degrees in theology, together with a fellow's certificate of the *Humboldt Stiftung*. No doctor's degree in education as yet: I am still working on a dissertation to be presented at a German university.

As I am sitting here trying to explain how I became what I am, I realize that for years I have been striving to understand exactly how one becomes the human being he is, in order to find out how he could perhaps manage to become a different human being who would be like he would want to be. I feel like blaming a few institutions and persons for not having allowed me to become all I wanted to be. I realize, however, that becoming or not the human being I want to be depends on me deciding what I want to be and using the means at my disposal to become that human being. At the same time I know that I must understand the process by which I have become who I am, in order to be able to help others, namely my students, become the human beings they want to be and act as they are expected as educators of other human beings. This means that, in my understanding, the study of education is of one piece with the reflection on the process of my own becoming.

Since I had the desire of learning how to write, and teachers as well as manuals on style encouraged me to start writing, I have kept a journal for years. I have written down experiences and observations. As I realize now, this procedure has kept me alert to changes that were happening with and around me. Writing this text today is like a summarizing the journal.

As I write this story it is as if I were placing myself before me through the words I write. We can in fact tell ourselves and others who we are only through words. Looking at the words we say about ourselves, we may come to a better realization of who we are or think we are.

In my case this process of becoming is not open-ended. It has a horizon, the kingdom of God, and moves toward a goal, to be and act as the kind of person the kingdom requires: trusting in God, loving toward the neighbor, and caring for all of creation.

How then do I perceive here and now, from this point and moment, how I came to be what I presume to be and to do what I think am doing? I believe we will find the answer if we consider the family and the circumstances--especially the schools in which I was brought up.

Family

The family into which I was born was a Lutheran pastor's family. At that time (1942) father served over a dozen congregations of German extraction in the Northwest plateau of Rio Grande do Sul, Brazil's southernmost state. I grew up in a beautiful country of rolling hills. It comprises forests and prairies, including the native araucaria pine tree. Today the scenery is determined by wheat, corn, and soybean plantations. Fifty years back the roads were narrow, dusty and full of potholes. Most of the traveling -- at least in our family -- was done by wagon and on horseback. Truck, bus and train were used only for larger trips.

25

Since father spent the years of the Second World War in prison, unjustly accused of having conspired against Brazil, I grew up under the care of my mother together with her parents, who lived with us. Grandfather and grandmother had come to Brazil with their only daughter after the First World War. They had settled in Cruz Machado, a government settlement in the State of Parana in South Brazil. There father met mother, and they got married.

Grandmother and especially grandfather used to tell me children's stories, the German Maerchen. They also told me about the zoo they used to visit in Germany, about the good food they used to eat, and about the brothers, sisters, nephews and nieces they had left in Wuppertal and other German cities. Grandfather would also take me along for walks in the forests and fields. He called my attention to trees and plants, telling me whether the fruit was good to eat, and the leaves or roots were good for curing ailments. He also collected stones and tried to find a special meaning in images he saw or imagined in them. I realize now that the Oma's and Opa's stories excited my imagination, developed my taste for literature, and provoked a longing for distant lands. As the years went by I had the privilege of reading good literature and of living in the United States and in Germany, besides visiting these countries several times on business and study trips.

After the war and its hysteria were over, my father was released from prison. He accepted an invitation to work in a Lutheran parish located farther Northwest in the Missoes area by the margins of the Ijuí river. His responsibilities included serving two congregations and taking care of a parochial school in the main congregation. This is how he, my father and pastor, also became my (first and only) elementary teacher. There I began to learn Portuguese both at play and in school.

Schooling

In school I learned fast and easy. At home I studied German. I learned to read and write in Gothic script. Father would read daily from the German Bible (with pictures!) at breakfast and supper. It had pictures (woodcuts). Each Sunday we were in church. I learned to play the violin, but never got too far with it. Later on I learned to play the organ and the piano. By the end of the third school year I was helping father in teaching reading to the younger pupils.

After five years of elementary school, the options were limited. I had the choice of remaining in the colony with nothing special to do, or of studying in the seminary of the Lutheran church in Porto Alegre. My parents did not have money to send me to the high school in the city nearby. At that time only rich people could afford that. So I find myself--barely eleven years old--in a boarding school in the State capital, Porto Alegre. To make a long story short, I spent eleven years in this school, as a high school student, seminarian, and intern.

As I was studying theology, however, I also enrolled in philosophy at the Federal University in Porto Alegre. The tuition was free, and the classes were held in the afternoon. I might have studied classical languages, but the Federal University offered this program in the morning only, when I had the theology classes. The Catholic University offered classical languages in the afternoon, but my family did not have money to pay for it.

For some reason as yet unknown I liked the classes on the history of education in the theology curriculum. In the last semesters of philosophy we took courses in educational psychology and pedagogy. I liked them very much and did a good job in teaching practice, as the (women) professors certified.

Teaching

Many years later, after having lived abroad and earned a doctor's degree in systematic theology, I applied and began teaching history of education part-time at the college in the city of Ijuí, where I was working. A few years later I was invited to serve as full-time executive of the Department of Education of a Lutheran church body in Brazil. My responsibilities included supervising a theological seminary, and several high and elementary schools.

As I returned to Germany in 1984 to revise, expand, and publish my doctoral dissertation, I registered in the pedagogical faculty of the local university, earned credits, arranged for an advisor, and chose a dissertation topic. Upon returning to Brazil I accepted an invitation to work as academic superintendent of the Lutheran colleges that were later expanded and transformed into the Lutheran University. This work, however, was mainly administrative, and I longed to teach in the classroom. Therefore I applied and was accepted as a part-time professor in the master's (and later the doctorate) program in education at the Catholic University in Porto Alegre.

How then did I become a teacher of teachers? Partly by chance and opportunity, but most of all by following the lead of a desire or intuition which suggests that this is what I would like to do, that this is what I am good at, and that this is what I find meaning, satisfaction, and joy in doing.

27

What is it that excites me? It is understanding the process of human history and society as a whole, and education as the edge and meeting of the old and new generations. Above all, however, what excites me is perceiving the possibilities that slumber in the students and helping them perceive and realize their possibilities. In other words, helping them realize and become the human beings they want to and can be--and motivating and empowering them to help others, their pupils and students, become the human beings they intend to be--all of this to create a society that will realize more fully our dreams of justice and well-being for all.

In order to make a long story short let me tell you that I end up working as a teacher of education for two reasons: I like it, and this seems to be a pleasant way of maintaining the family and myself--and a way of contributing for the well being of human beings and the good of creation.

The Joys Of Being A Teacher: My Story

Anicia A. Alvarez
Brunei Darussalam

My country, the Philippines, is a string of 1400 islands in the Western Pacific known for its scenic countryside, and for its friendly and cheerful people. Zamboanga, the city where I was born is located in one of the country's largest islands, Mindanao. Dubbed as the city of flowers and noted for the Hispanic beauty of its maidens, the city and the countryside are splattered with an abundant array of bougainvillea lining the city streets and private homes, lush towering hundred years old acacia trees and to tempt one's critical taste and palate, an abundance of fresh fish and sea foods daily caught from the sea bordering the city's coast. A songwriter aptly summarises the beauty of the city in an old song which is still the favourite of school children, "don't you go to far Zamboanga for you may forget your darling far away."

Born prematurely in 1945 when the American forces were liberating the city from the Japanese Imperial Army, my parents were helped by a generous American soldier, Corporal Dixon, who gave my mother a shoe box and GI blankets to wrap and warm my whole body of 5 lbs. Mr. Dixon later became a close family friend whose parents in the U.S. sent my mother baby clothes, Gerber baby food, and American chocolates. After the war, Mr. Dixon used to send me American books and magazines which strengthened our family ties and influenced my early education and learning in later years a great deal.

I come from a humble family of educators. My grandmother was a teacher trained under the Spanish Cartilla method of teaching. My mother attended school under the Japanese Imperial system of education. When the Americans liberated the city, schooling became compulsory in public schools under the supervision of American educators. Secondary schooling was at the Zamboanga Normal School, one of the teacher training schools established all over the country by the Thomasites, the first American teachers so-called because they came aboard an American ship the SS Thomas. Built in 1922, this normal school now a university, still stands intact and complete even after the ravages of two world wars. Completion of secondary education at this prestigious school qualified my mother to become one of the first teachers to teach in English during and after the American occupation.

My schooling was strongly influenced by the American school system where the Star Spangled Banner was sang every morning together with the Philippine National Anthem during flag raising ceremony. My generation went through a 6-4-4 formal education of primary, secondary and tertiary schooling following a curriculum marked by a strong influence of American history and literature and a compulsory learning of the Spanish language and culture. And who can forget the two immortal novels of our national hero Dr. Jose Rizal, the Noli Me Tan Gere and El Filibusterismo, whose interpretation and understanding we had to portray in the eloquence of dramatics and short plays. There was also the poem Mi Ultimo Adios (My Last Farewell) written on the eve of Rizal's execution by the Spaniards and whose 23 stanzas we had to recite in class.

To be a teacher was not my first choice. I was ambitious, gregarious, talented, and bright. I wanted to travel and visit all the places in America that pervaded our learning in schools. As a teacher all this would seem highly unlikely. I wanted first of all to pursue a medical career and specialise as a heart surgeon in one of the prestigious hospital in America. This was not practical for we could not afford the exorbitant fees of training in medicine. I settled to pursue a course in nursing. I was already on to my sophomore year when unfortunately, my mother had to undergo a major tumor operation of the head which left her paralyzed up to the present time. Besides, I realised that as the eldest in the family, the responsibility of looking after three brothers and two younger sisters rested primarily on me, especially after the demise of my father.

After high school I went on to complete a two year certificate programme and was awarded an Elementary Teachers' Certificate (ETC) that qualified me to teach in the primary grades. My first teaching experience was a multi-grade class of Yakan children (an ethnic tribe in Basilan Island) in a rural school. These children, who had never seen and experienced city life, provided me with joy, satisfaction, and self-fulfillment where the first seed of commitment as a teacher took place in my heart and set priority over all other interests. From the start, I knew that I had a responsibility to these kids, and that I had to keep their enthusiasm to learn the rudiments of reading, writing, and arithmetic alive in their youthful countenance and expressions. I knew I had to nurture and protect their love for schooling because these were the very few children on whom the improvement and development of their ethnic culture and survival depended. My initial training in music and art education was most useful and significant for I did a lot of expressive art work, music and play with the children. I found out that, no matter how well I prepared teaching plans, I could not always follow them. Instead one was guided by one's philosophy and common sense when it came to facing the children day after day. There were no writing notebooks nor books to follow. I had to rely on my former teachers for materials on what to teach and critically observe classes in session during seminars and workshops. I remember taking my pupils to the local river and forest and teaching them about plants and animals, and in return, learning from the children about life in the mountains. I remember the interest and eagerness of the children during story telling time, their desire to learn spelling and arithmetic, and their youthful expressions during games, art and music. And when parents gifted me with their simple generosity of fruits, live chickens and vegetables in appreciation for what I was doing for the children, I was encouraged and ever more committed with a renewed vitality and vigour.

The impact of this experience was stimulating enough for me to go back to the city and get the necessary teacher training qualifications to give me the security and permanent status to make teaching my career. I also had the foresight that an Elementary Teachers Certificate would someday be outdated as more and more students avail of tertiary education. By this time the world was excited about the race to conquer the moon by the United States and Russia and I was just fascinated by

Sputnik, Gagarin, Tereshkova and the advances made in space exploration. It took me three years of professional training to qualify for a teaching position in the primary school. I continued my professional schooling for another two years to complete a secondary education degree specialising in two subject areas in the secondary school curriculum, physical science and biological science.

I became a high school science teacher at one of the largest public schools in the city topping the competitive examination used in the screening and selection of teacher applicants. My first four years of teaching first year high school students in the lowest sections in Zamboanga City High School were full of interesting events and satisfying experiences. Teachers often complained when assigned to teach sections K to O or sections 10 to 12. In terms of academic ability, these students scored the lowest amongst their peers. Teachers do not want to teach these classes. To my satisfaction, I found teaching general science to these students both interesting and challenging. At one foundation day celebration my classes set up a mock-up of the moon surface, a NASA monitoring station and an Apollo spaceship hovering on top of the moon and ending up with Armstrong landing on the moon. I listened to my students and as I listened more, they also listened and talked less and I adjusted my behaviour towards them accordingly. I had a great rapport with the young and older students alike, made home visits when pupils were absent, talked with parents during the once-a-month homeroom PTA day and most of all experienced the human feelings of anger, joy, resentment and enthusiasm exhibited by the 40 different and unique personalities in the classroom. I treated these students as they were, rather than what they ought to be, and my expectations of them were realistic according to each ones ability and maturity. The same feeling of commitment that I had with my first ethnic group of pupils pervaded in my heart for these first year students classified by the schools' examination system as "underachievers."

After four years of fruitful teaching, I realised that if I were to make a greater impact on the lives of young students, I had to become more than just a classroom teacher. I had to reach out to 'teacher trainees' whose training I felt I must enrich with qualities that would excite children to learn and perform well beyond normal expectations.

I went to graduate school, teaching during the day time and studying in the evening. It took me two years of part time and two summers of graduate study to complete a Master's Degree in Science Education. With a master's degree I joined the teacher training faculty of the Zamboanga State College. Two years later, I was awarded a Fulbright scholarship to pursue doctoral studies at Purdue University where I had the opportunity to work with prominent educators like F. Nordland, J. B. Kahle, D. Herron, S. Postlewait, H. Jaus, and C. Hicks. I shall always remember my scholastic contacts with them with much fondness.

My training at Purdue University was the highlight of my career. This was the time when the emphasis on education reform was to improve student learning of academic content and "excellence" in academic work. I was in the midst of a reform movement where teachers and teacher training were to go through a development of education studies of core courses that would enhance knowledge, varied teaching techniques, work habits that should entail inquiry and problem solving skills, collegiality and self-evaluation and reflection. I was prepared and trained to do just that, working myself through biological sciences content courses, pedagogical and methods courses, curriculum planning and implementation and a good grounding of research and statistics. After four years of doctoral study, I returned to my University with a deeper resolve to contribute towards an educated society and help teachers build a better and a strong Philippine nation.

I was appointed Director of the University's Research Center while at the same time continued teaching in the Faculty of Education and graduate school. By this time, teacher training for the Bachelor of Elementary Education was more oriented to Philippine values, culture, and traditions. Professional courses were balanced with arts courses in Philippine culture and history. Subject matter content was afforded for all subjects in the elementary school curriculum. The curriculum for the Bachelor of Science in Education was more or less the same except for the emphasis on the development of the Filipino adolescent, a grounding of content in the two chosen areas of specialisation, but balanced with courses in English and Filipino communication skills and a foreign language. Where before pedagogical and methods of teaching courses constituted only a small fraction of units in the teacher training curriculum, a review of the programmes placed emphasis on pedagogical studies and the "how to do it" courses more than philosophy, psychology and school management. Field experience or practice teaching became an important element in the programmes as research findings made it more explicit that performance in theory-based courses accounted for only a small proportion of variation in student teaching performance. In-campus practice teaching for one semester was done in a

33

Laboratory School under the guidance and supervision of critic teachers and practice teaching supervisors. This was followed by another semester of off-campus teaching where trainees were assigned to local schools under the supervision of cooperating teachers.

In the course of my methods courses where competencies and skills are internalised and modeled, I usually like to recount to my teacher trainees my own classroom experiences as a beginning teacher. I also recount the reasons why I stayed as a teacher and my philosophy on why I teach the way I do. I often reflect and discuss with them the ever strong influence my former teachers had on me especially in the early years of my schooling. For example, Mrs. Santillana, my Grade I teacher, provided us with happy memories of learning how to read and write and cultivating in us respect for the elders. My self-concept was strengthened by the success I had, coming home on the last day of the school year with 100 pages of written lessons all marked 100%. I learned to love science through my grade IV teacher, Mr. Artesano. He taught us basic science concepts through his innovative ideas for outdoor simple experiments and improvised materials. For us to discover the boiling temperature of water remaining constant at 100 degree Celsius, no matter how long it boils, was something that we talked about in amazement for many days. Or my first year high school science teacher, Mrs. Vicente, who taught us the rudiments of inquiry and logical thinking. Through her intuitive and skillful questions, I was able to explain why wooden house fences were painted or why we heard the roar of the thunder first and then saw the lightning in the sky.

Although teachers get inspiration from others, I expose my teacher trainees to the idea that each of them will eventually have a personal philosophy that will form the foundation of their professional decisions. After all, isn't the whole process of teaching preparation, planning, implementation and evaluation a matter of making professional decisions? This philosophy generated from their experiences in life, professional upbringing and experiences in the teacher training programme has to do with the beliefs and values of the teaching culture they would expouse about the teaching and learning process. Teachers with strong beliefs and values about how children learn are constantly reflecting on the things they do, facing each class every school year with thoughts that each new group presents, new challenges and opportunities. They are constantly enriching their knowledge enlivened by the fact that life is a process of constant change and that the teacher responsibility is to

34

provide the appropriate experiences and the opportunities for each child to fully develop his/her potential. Good teachers focus their instruction on important content covering less but in greater depth, emphasize higher order thinking skills that stress understanding and application of concepts, and making fewer tradeoffs between important content and convenience.

I enjoy supervising students during in-campus and off-campus observation, getting acquainted with cooperating teachers, observing classroom situations, and talking with school headmasters on ways on how beginning teachers can be assisted. I conduct in-service training and assist in the professional up grading of teachers. As more of the actual classroom situations are seen and more discussions and interactions shared with those in actual teaching, I continue to excel in classroom action research or research projects. Research keeps my interest and involvement with the teaching profession alive and contacts with other academics working in the same areas intensifies this interest and enthusiasm. Consultancies with agencies outside the university complete my teaching/research/extension functions mandated of a university academic. In 1987 I joined the Faculty of Education of the University of Brunei Darussalam as a curriculum specialist in education. The requirements and expectations for developing teacher professionals are more or less the same as in other Southeast Asian countries. Training preservice teachers in this rich monarchical country is no different from the teacher training programmes I was associated with back home. The emphasis continues to remain on strengthening the personal qualities of teacher trainees, advocating enjoyment when teaching, looking forward to being with students, achieving self-fulfillment and commitment in their work, being flexible and dynamic to adapt to changes and acquiring the necessary professional preparation and communication skills to make decisions when planning for the teaching-learning process.

My experiences as an educator, supervisor and administrator at my former University were useful when I was appointed Deputy Dean and, now, Dean of Faculty of Education at UBD. With this post came the responsibility of reviewing the teacher training programmes offered by the Faculty amidst new reforms and policies of bilingual education. The programme review and evaluation process of the programmes by an international community of scholars eventually produced a revised primary education programme structure for training teachers to work successfully in a country espousing bilingual education. The programme places

35

emphasis on "pedagogical content knowledge" where interactions between what is taught and how best it can be taught are linked; the need for teacher trainees to critique their own practice; and to be dynamic, learning by doing, reading and watching others. Reflecting back on being a classroom teacher since 1966 and now an educator of teachers, I believe strongly that good teachers can only benefit from good committed educators while the reverse is true for non-committed and non-caring educators.

Profile Of A Secondary Teacher Educator In Cameroon

Leke Tambo
Cameroon

Introduction

This profile of a secondary teacher educator in Cameroon is based, for the most part, on my life story and activities. It written as part of an international comparative study on who teacher educators are and the pathways through which they have acquired their positions in teacher education.

Apart from responding to this global need, the description could throw some light on the current debate about the competencies and role expectations of secondary teacher educators in Cameroon. This debate relates to efforts aimed at improving secondary teacher education in the country, and was identified as an area of study during a Cameroon-Canada inter-university seminar held in July-August 1992.

The "Story" which follows is presented in terms of the following headings: (1) my status; or who I am, (2) my place and nature of work, (3) my educational preparation, and (4) other information. Although the story is based on my personal experience, attempts are made to relate it to the experience of the typical Cameroon secondary teacher educator.

My Status, or Who I Am

I was born in 1951, in the small village of Lewoh in Lebialem Division of Cameroon. I am married, with four children. My career in teacher education spans a period of over seventeen years and mainly involves secondary teacher education.

My Place and Nature of Work

I worked at the Higher Teachers' College (Ecole Normale Superieure, ENS) of the University of Yaounde. ENS, as the institution is commonly known in Cameroon, was founded in 1961, being the first of the institutions of the University of Yaounde to receive its charter.

The mission of ENS was to prepare secondary school teachers and teachers of primary-level teacher training institutions. I taught these two categories of student teachers. The average age of the first category was 20 and that of the second 25 years.

Training objectives emphasized: (1) acquisition of subject matter in the students' chosen subject areas, (2) knowledge about educational foundations (psychology, sociology, philosophy, and other education courses), (3) knowledge about pedagogy (general and specific teaching methods and strategies), and (4) applying all of this knowledge in a teaching-learning situation.

While many of my colleagues in the different departments concentrated their effort on the first objective, the professional education department focused attention on the last three objectives. Thus the first year courses emphasized foundational issues in education, those of the second year dealt mainly with pedagogy, school management, and administration. In the third year, the main concern was to help students apply this knowledge in teaching. So, students spent some time in the schools practicing in the classrooms.

When students were on vacation, I was expected to do a variety of things related to my status as a university faculty member. These ranged from research and writing, participation in workshops and seminars, to community service activities. These were expectations of the university and I made every effort to respond positively to them.

For a number of years I had participated in at least two seminars each year within the framework of the Cooperation Project between ENS and the University of Regina (Canada). I had organized workshops and seminars involving my colleagues, cooperating teachers, and Cameroon Ministry of Education authorities. Additionally, I did research and published in a number of international journals on education. I served on the review board of some educational journals and also served as a resource person to teachers and researchers within my community.

Many of my colleagues liked to do these things and were quite busy during their free time. But some seem to prefer doing things such as recreation and small business enterprises to increase their family incomes. I expect that in the coming years the number of my colleagues involved in such ventures will increase, unless the economic situation of the country improves.

After a number of years at ENS, I accepted a position as Assocaite to the Vice Chancellor. I am responsible for international relationships for the University of Buea. I still maintain an indirect involvement with teacher education, for I feel that the preparation of good teachers is essential to the well being of my country.

My Educational Preparation

The pathway through which I became a secondary teacher educator is as follows: After my elementary school course, I trained as a primary school teacher for five years. This initial teacher education program included acquisition of subject matter related to all the subjects of the elementary school curriculum, as well as teaching skills and attitudes. After graduation from the elementary or primary teacher training college, I taught briefly in a primary school and then went to an advanced secondary school where I did a two year university preparatory course leading to the General Certificate of Education-Advanced Level.

With this qualification I was admitted in the university for a Bachelor of Arts degree program in history, with minors in geography and sociology. Upon graduation I was admitted in a faculty of education where I studied for a master and doctoral degrees in education.

The above pathway is typical of many of my colleagues who teach in departments of professional education.

For the departments that are more academic than professionally oriented, the typical pathway involves an elementary school course, five years of secondary and two years of advanced secondary school course, a bachelor, master and doctoral degrees in a specific discipline.

As it can readily be seen, faculty who have followed the different pathways complement each other in the secondary teacher education program. This is specifically so for the first cycle program where trainee's entry qualification is expected to be only a secondary school graduation certificate and so there is need for the trainees to acquire, during the training period, higher levels of subject matter in their respective fields of specialization.

At the second cycle of the secondary teacher education program where candidates are expected to have obtained the bachelor's degree or its equivalent in their proposed subject of teaching, the pathway that emphasizes academics becomes less useful to youngsters who are already well grounded in the content of their disciplines. Partly for this reason, recruitment policy for secondary teacher educators now emphasizes competence in both academic and professional knowledge. As well, staff development policy is giving some attention to the professional training of academic-oriented faculty in the basic principles of teaching and evaluation of student learning.

I personally feel that these changing expectations of the secondary teacher educator in Cameroon are a welcome development because through these expectations many of my colleagues will be encouraged to complement their academic knowledge with pedagogic and professional knowledge.

Other Information

As indicated above there are two categories of teacher educators in Cameroon: secondary teacher educators and primary teacher educators. The former prepares teachers for the secondary general, secondary technical and primary teacher education institutions, while the latter prepares primary school teachers.

Whereas the foregoing story focused on the secondary teacher educator, it may be interesting here to relate it to the experience of primary teacher educators.

Typically, secondary teacher educators are university lecturers or professors and their minimum qualification is a master's degree. The majority of them have earned a doctoral degree in their area of specialization. By comparison, primary teacher educators are expected to possess only the bachelor's degree or its equivalent, since primary school teaching in Cameroon does not require a university degree. However, owing to the phenomenon of "qualification inflation" it is becoming common to find people with master's and doctoral degrees teaching in these institutions.

In terms of their nature of work, these people often teach a variety of subjects in the "academic" and "professional" disciplines and so the gap between these disciplines is not as emphasized at this level as it is at the secondary teacher education level. They teach their students to know the relevant content and pedagogy

40

for all the subjects of the primary school curriculum since primary school teachers are expected to teach all of these subjects to the grades or classes they are assigned.

In general, one would say that primary teacher educators are often more prepared for the work they do, and tend to be more conscientious in doing their work than most secondary teacher educators who tend to limit their teaching to one curriculum area and emphasize subject matter acquisition even to the detriment of pedagogic and professional knowledge.

Adventures of Becoming a Canadian Teacher Educator

LeOra Cordis
Canada

Career and life shift

The early morning light softened the Idaho landscape as I stopped within sight of the Canadian border crossing. I needed a few minutes for reflection and closure before I crossed into Canada. Yesterday I had left a 26 year marriage that had evolved from turbulent to destructive. Today I would leave the country of my birth, my culture, my environment, my family and my life as I had known it for 43 years. I would go to a country foreign to me; to a city filled with strangers; to a university I had visited once--all of this to do a job I had never done before. With a mixture of apprehension and anticipation I drove to Customs, declared my meager settler's effects and launched onto the adventure of becoming a Canadian teacher educator.

Early life and teaching experiences

My life began on a winter day in 1929. My childhood consisted of roaming the creeks, meadows and hills on our ranch with my two older brothers. My early education was a one-room school (K-grade 8) in the Nebraska Sandhills. Upon entering high school my intent was to become a pilot and join the military to ferry planes. My parents weren't of the same mind; thus, I took a two year normal training course that was a "stream" at the local high school. At the completion of this course I received a Nebraska Teaching Certificate after passing examinations set by the State Department of Education. In September 1945, at the age of 16, I started teaching in a one-room rural school. With the exception of 5 years, I would be a professional educator for the next 49 years.

A mixture of teaching, marriage, raising a child, going to school and being active in community was my life for the several years it took to finally attain my B. Ed. degree from Chadron State College (Nebraska) in 1962. A few years experience in a city system had prompted me to return to rural teaching prior to attaining my B.Ed. I liked the "wholeness" of teaching--where else could one be superintendent, principal, teacher, secretary, coach, custodian, librarian, curriculum developer, playground supervisor, and everything else all at once? I liked the freedom to approach education from a "start where the child is" basis and the interdependence and cooperation demanded of children in a multiage setting.

Like most classroom teachers, one of the most important life lessons I learned was from children. Ten or twelve children, mostly boys, ages 5-12 liked to play football during recess and noon hour. Loud, rough disputes were common. I told them to settle their disagreements in a more civil manner or they could not play football. My warning had no impact and one day I cut short their play time, supervising them as they sat quietly in their desks. When they resumed normal movement, one 12 year old went to the library corner, got a football rule book, laid it before me and declared, "Read this and you'll be the referee and we can play football." His reasoning was that because I didn't know how to play football was no reason they shouldn't play. He was right. I did read the rule book and with their help on clarifying terms we continued to play football. Each child accepted that I did not know football, yet they could teach me enough to enable us to live and play together in a compatible, enjoyable manner. I normally involved children in peer teaching yet this was the first time I had experienced students intentionally and consciously teaching the teacher. Those children taught me all I know about football, but more important they taught me that combining knowledge and experiences of unlikely human combinations could be beneficial for everyone involved.

When our daughter graduated from high school in 1964 we decided to abandon the cold Nebraska winters and move to Oregon. For the next 5 years I taught kindergarten in a logging community. I also took graduate classes at the University of Oregon. In 1969 I decided to become a full time graduate student. I was a Graduate Fellow at the University of Oregon, which means I taught graduate and undergraduate classes and supervised practica. Due to officially completing my

M.Ed. with the written Ph.D. exams, I obtained both the M.Ed. and Ph.D. in 1972. After the usual job search and interviews, I decided to go the University of Saskatchewan, Regina Campus because it was a young university and offered career opportunities. Regina is the capital of Saskatchewan situated amidst the agricultural wealth of the prairies. Its population in 1972 was 125,000 and had grown to over 170,000 by 1994.

Canadian Experiences

The University of Saskatchewan, Regina Campus--which later became the University of Regina, was established in 1964. It was a combination of a local Teachers College and Liberal Arts College. In 1972 the enrollment in the university was nearly 6,000 students with about 1,000 of them in the Faculty of Education. When I retired in 1994 the enrollment was over 12,000, with 4,000 plus in Education programs. In 1972 the Faculty of Education had a staff of approximately 50. It was a mixture of staff from the Teachers College and "new blood," many from Britain and the United States. It was an exciting, interesting mix of cultures and philosophies coming together to establish quality teacher education programs within the university. When I retired in 1994 the established staff remained about 50 with additional sessional and term appointments.

When I interviewed for a position in the Faculty of Education, the Dean shared with me the possibility of a liaison with the Saskatchewan Department of Education. The focus of this liaison was kindergarten pilot sites. He also expressed a goal of expanding the early childhood program. These were two challenging opportunities I was confident were within my professional realm. In addition to my duties at the university, I was kindergarten consultant with the Saskatchewan Department of Education for four years. My rural childhood and teaching experiences were great assets for this role. During this period the Saskatchewan Legislature revised the Education Act. I had major influence in wording the portion establishing provincial funded kindergartens.

When I arrived at the University of Regina in 1972, the provincial requirement for teacher certification was a one year program. The revision in the Education Act that brought kindergartens to Saskatchewan also extended teacher education to three years, with a proviso to extend the requirements to four years. During my first years in Canada a small, collaborative cadre of us conducted experimental elementary groups built on the philosophy of supportive, field based

45

teacher education. I was a critical influence in this program development and ensured a strong early childhood component was embedded in the elementary program. I designed several early childhood courses and was involved in the development of the required Professional Studies course. Over the years I taught early childhood, child development and professional studies courses in our campus, extension and Native Teacher Education programs. The elementary program became a model for other programs within our faculty. The portions modeled were the involvement of field personnel on advisory and working committees regarding program development and field experiences; a strong "theory into practice" within the professional development and curriculum courses; off-campus residential experiences relating classroom experiences with local heritages, history and nature; a personal theory base prior to extended practica; and a 16 week (semester) of extended practica. Involvement of field personnel was an integral part of our program--they made our program stronger and being involved made all of us stronger.

Although deeply involved in the elementary program I recognized the inservice teachers' need for a graduate program in early childhood. I helped shape a broad M. Ed. program at the University of Regina that enabled students to focus in their chosen areas. Many field teachers enrolled in our early childhood courses and often persons not in early childhood would join us, especially in the assessment course.

My role as university professor was the usual teaching, research and writing for journals. I chose to extend that role to include program development; field research and writing that refined the elementary and early childhood programs; serving on university committees; being director of the Children's Center, located in the Education Building; and remaining active in local, national and international professional organizations. In my role as director I developed and implemented two programs within the Children's Center. One program was to select teachers from local school units and provide them a supportive environment to try new or different teaching styles. The other program was to train paraprofessionals. Due to my involvement with International Society for Teacher Educators I came to understand other education systems and was better able to contribute to innovations within our programs.

I have the dubious honor of several "firsts" at the University of Regina's Faculty of Education. Keep in mind that "firsts" take the brunt of much, therefore, smoothing the trail for those that follow--thus the notion of dubious honor. Within the Faculty of Education I was the first female Ph.D., first female full professor, one of three to teach the first professional studies course, first to try out new program concepts and probably other firsts I don't want to remember.

I became a Canadian citizen when the U.S. allowed its citizens to hold dual citizenship. My years as a Canadian teacher educator were filled with program development, supervision, research, writing, field liaison, and much hearty involvement with my colleagues. Living in conservative Saskatchewan with its social programs had an interesting effect on a comparatively liberal me. I became more liberal in my view of responsibilities to others.

Retirement

The early morning light softened the Canadian Rockies as I stopped within sight of the American border crossing. I needed a few minutes for reflection before I crossed into the States. At this border crossing nearly 22 years earlier I had started to carve a new life for myself. I didn't know then how many times a divorced American female with a Ph.D. would have to prove herself credible. I had also learned about head-bolt, interior, and battery heaters to get your car started and those fur coats really aren't a foolish luxury in some climates. I had come to realize how versatile I could be, how I could surprise myself so many times with the result of "Yes, let's give that a try." I had come to love the broad expanse and sky of flat Saskatchewan. I had the satisfaction of my constant striving to teach in a manner that allowed student's learning. I couldn't recall how many times I said to myself, "I'm never going to drive in a white-out blizzard again. Well, not at night anyway." I could hardly believe the whole world contained as many fine people as I had come to know, and especially how many of them would populate my life when I needed support and friendship. In that early morning light I recognized how fulfilling and satisfying my life as a Canadian teacher educator had been. With nostalgia I drove to Customs, declared my settler's effects and launched onto the adventure of becoming a retired teacher educator.

The Story Of How I Became A Teacher Educator

Jan Trojak
Czech Republic

I was born in 1936 in Prague. Now, at the end of my professional career, I am still here, in my birthplace, acting as a Docent (equivalent to an Associate Professor) at the Department of Didactics of Mathematics of the Faculty of Mathematics and Physics of the ancient Charles' University (founded in 1348 by the Roman Emperor and Czech King, Charles the Fourth).

I graduated in 1961 from the Science Faculty of the Pedagogical University in Prague, becoming a secondary school teacher specialized in mathematics and descriptive geometry. The Pedagogical University was established in 1953 to educate secondary school teachers for all the school-subjects. Prospective teachers of the junior classes of a secondary school followed a 3 year program. Those who wanted to teach at senior classes studied a different 4 year program. Teacher educators were recruited for this new university mostly from the specialists in the science or the art associated with the particular school subject, who also had enough experience in the secondary school teaching. Many of those who lectured in mathematics were authors of mathematics textbooks, not only for the secondary schools, but also for the mathematics teachers. Some of these books I still use and appreciate.

I was studying very well, owing more to the fact that I was about three or four years older than my university schoolmates, than to talent of any kind. How this came about and why I have chosen the profession of a mathematics teacher could not be well understood without a digression into the events which happened when I was fifteen.

When in 1951, at the time of the strictest communist rule, I was leaving the lower secondary school and the decision should have been made, whether I qualified for the further education at a senior secondary school (called "gymnasium"), my chances were hindered by my bad record. I was labeled "the child of the religious family" and any further study was denied to me.

I was expelled from the district, worked for two years as the gardener's apprentice, got a certificate and worked for another year as a journeyman in a garden. During these three years of the manual work I found time enough to learn English, mathematics and descriptive geometry. Often, doing monotonous work, I would learn English phrases or mathematical formulae. I was lucky in encountering two excellent teachers, both prematurely (for their respective "reactionary" opinions) retired secondary school teachers. They taught me mathematics and English in their respective homes, during the period of my gardening and even for some years after. Their teaching methods were original and effective; we never studied English grammar as such--we simply read books, the first one was the *Fairy Tales* by Oscar Wilde; most of geometry we discussed in the complete darkness or with our eyes closed (no computers--by the way--at that time).

In 1953, the imperative "class struggle" relinquished a little and in 1954 I was admitted mercifully to the higher classes of the secondary school to complete my study. My knowledge of mathematics and descriptive geometry was rather advanced when I entered the secondary school again, and I was bored by mathematics as a school subject. Though still interested in the advanced topics of mathematics and above all in its applications I was not about to be a mathematician. My dream was to become a physician. Involved in the voluntary work of the Red Cross I was enthusiastically preparing myself to enter Medical Faculty to be, preferably, a pediatrician.

When time came to apply for the entry to the university, my teachers (many of whom did not conceal their sympathy) had discouraged me from applying for the Medical Faculty with my unfavourable record and urged me to study mathematics instead, where much lower number of applicants was expected. And so I did. I was accepted to study mathematics and descriptive geometry at the Faculty of Science of the Pedagogical University.

After I graduated in 1961 I applied for and I got the post of an assistant at the Department of Algebra and Geometry (headed by an excellent scholar and academician Prof. Korinek). There I became an assistant to Prof. Vysín, the former head of the Department of Mathematics at the Pedagogical University, transferred to the Faculty of Mathematics and Physics to assist in the development of teacher education. By accepting the post, I already predetermined the orientation of my future career to the teacher education.

Besides guiding exercises on college algebra and geometry I was bound to work in one of the mathematics research group (it was the graph theory group I chose at that time) and to teach mathematics in two regular classes of the secondary school with all the duties pertaining to this work. After three "introductory" years I was appointed a lecturer; my duties extended gradually to lectures on projective, non-Euclidean and elementary geometries and to a more extensive study of mathematics with the aim to reach the C.Sc.(equivalent to Ph.D.) degree in an unspecified time. It was expected, tacitly, that I would educate myself to become a competent teacher of mathematics to the prospective teachers of mathematics of the higher classes of the secondary schools.

Since 1967 the relaxation of the political climate started, aimed to give way to some moderate changes in private undertaking and to ease the economy of the growing difficulties. Also the permissions to leave the country and work abroad were granted abundantly. Recommended by one of my colleagues I was invited by the University of Basrah (Iraq) to read lectures on non-Euclidean and projective geometries, starting from the academic year 1968-69.

During the five years I spent in Persian Gulf, I learned a lot of things, many of them without a direct bearing to the teacher education, but the majority of them contributing to my general intellectual maturity. I came to know many genuine men of various nationalities. The University of Basrah was a young institution (founded about 1964) and its staff was international. The College of Science provided only the B.Sc. degree and the brightest of students there were easily getting scholarships to study at European and American universities. The rest of them went to teach science at secondary schools.

I learned many new parts of mathematics, while perfecting my knowledge of those which I thought I knew well. As a teacher from Europe, I was expected being able to read lecture on any topic of mathematics, not only for the College of Science, but also for the engineering colleges of various kinds. Although I may not have been an expert in a particular field, I used the little time I had to learn fast and to become an expert in time. The normal teaching load was about 15 hours per week, but there were semesters with the load exceeding 20. Despite the strange surroundings and an extremely hot climate (with temperature approaching 50 degrees centigrade in shade for at least four months of a year) I have sort of fallen for this mysterious oriental country, spending there long years of the most productive part of my life.

At the end of every academic year, the work of each of the foreign teachers had been evaluated by the university authorities before a decision was taken to extend the teacher's contract or not. I should have to confess that my self-confidence rose seeing my hard work appreciated. This was by no means every teacher's case.

I had to return back home to Czechoslovakia every year to ask the government and my faculty for the permission to extend my stay abroad for another year (I remained a permanent employee of my home faculty from which the leave without pay was granted to me). The most appreciated provision of my working abroad was the opportunity to travel. My earnings did not allow me any luxury, but with a tent and a second-hand car I went many times from Prague up to the Persian Gulf and back home again, enjoying the freedom of movement and learning all that I could of what I met along my way. This experience contributed very much to my competence of a teacher educator.

When I returned to Prague for good in 1975 I worked hard on my C.Sc. thesis--almost all my peers had either earned the title already or they were at the final stage of the study. In Fall of 1976, I submitted a study on differential geometry of a quaternionic space and passed the rigorous examination, getting the title R.N.Dr. At the end of 1977 I defended my C.Sc. thesis on the tangent structures of the three-dimensional submanifolds of the quaternionic space.

In the second half of the seventies, I was becoming more and more involved in the problems of the identification and fostering of the mathematically gifted pupils. At one of the senior secondary schools in Prague, special mathematical classes were situated, which was run as a boarding school for mathematically gifted students from all over Bohemia. To the first form, the selection of pupils (aged 15) was based on their results in mathematical competitions (like Mathematical Olympiad) and on the number of points gained in the written as well as oral 'talent' entrance examination. From 1975 until recently I taught in the last two forms of this special mathematical class from five to ten teaching-hours weekly, guiding seminar work on the advanced topics of mathematics and teaching programming in PASCAL. Many of the students of these classes used to come to our faculty to study mathematics or physics, sometimes even to be mathematics and/or physics teachers. I taught in that mathematical class for fifteen years and I still participate in the talent entrance examinations and in the final 'maturity' examinations. With a small group of my colleagues we used to research some problems connected with mathematical giftedness. More recently, we have involved ourselves strongly in the study of gender differences in the development of the mathematical talent.

In 1986 I was appointed a docent in the theory of education of mathematics.

I worked also as an administrator, heading the Section of Geometry of the Department of Didactics of Mathematics for five years. When a new teacher specialization was created, computer science (combined with mathematics or physics), I was appointed Head of the Section of Didactics of Computer Science of the same department. At present, I read lectures on analytic geometry and on non-Euclidean geometry for the prospective mathematics teachers. I am also guiding the seminar on the identification and fostering of the mathematical talent of the young people and the M.Sc. theses in mathematics and didactics of mathematics for the prospective mathematics teachers.

The Faculty of Mathematics and Physics was created by separation from the Faculty of Science as a further faculty of the Charles University in Prague in 1953. It comprises of many departments, formed for educational and research purposes and related to mathematics, physics computer science and many interdisciplinary sciences. Besides educating the specialists in sciences, offering B.Sc, M.Sc and Ph.D. programs, the faculty is also educating the secondary-school teachers in five-years M.Sc. program. Prospective teachers are studying a combination of two subjects (considered as major): mathematics with physics, descriptive geometry or computer science and physics with computer science. A student is obliged to conclude his study by writing a thesis in any subject of his combination.

There is no percentage determined by my institution for teaching, administrative or any other kind of work. It is expected that a docent or professor will hold from eight to ten hours of lectures, including one or two seminars usually related to his research work. In addition, teacher educators guide and review M.Sc. theses and supervise students when they are practicing in classes under the guidance of experienced secondary-school teachers. Together with the mathematicians-specialists the teacher educators are members of the examination committees (appointed by the Dean of the faculty) for the final state-examinations on mathematics and didactics of mathematics and for the defence of the M.Sc. theses of the students in the last, fifth year, prospective teachers.

Most of the administrative work is done by the secretary of the department, which recently has been facilitated by the computer network. What remains to be done by the educator is still felt as a burden. It is not regular work and its share would be very difficult--if not impossible--to express in percentage.

Every professor and docent is expected to participate in or conduct research in natural science or in didactics of his science and to publish his results. Teacher educators are often authors of textbooks for secondary-school students or for the education of teachers.

I am strongly convinced of the fact that the education of mathematics teachers is only successful, if students are taught mathematics by teachers, who not only are good mathematicians, but who also are experienced in secondary school teaching and who are also able to share their profound knowledge of mathematics with their students, keeping in mind in doing so, that they are instructing teachers. It is generally understood that a statistician needs a different concept of mathematics education than a computer scientist or a mathematician, who believes that research in pure mathematics will be his daily bread. Equally well, mathematics taught to a mathematics teacher-to-be should respect the main, very special purpose for which it is learned: to be transformed by the teacher into an appropriate age and intellectual level and then taught again by the teacher, while reflecting the circumstances under which he was hired to do so.

I am not advocating a complete separation of teacher education from the education of mathematical specialists. I believe that also a prospective teacher should come into contact with research in mathematics, particularly with an applied research. Teachers should be convinced in their pre-service education that the main reason why pupils have to learn mathematics lies in its applicability. For this reason, also the teacher educators lecturing on any mathematical topic, should have a profound, though perhaps broader knowledge of mathematics, compared with mathematical specialists, and should have a personal experience in a mathematics research of one kind or another.

In the sixties, prospective mathematics teachers could study at our faculty to become qualified in teaching either mathematics and physics, or mathematics and descriptive geometry at the higher classes of secondary schools for pupils aged 15 to 19. For the first two years, all the students enrolled into our faculty studied together, no matter in what branch of science they intended to specialize. Together with future mathematicians-specialists, physicists, meteorologists, astronomers, geophysicists and the like, the prospective teachers also were educated. Not earlier than at the end of the second year, students had to make their final decision and to apply for an admission into the desired specialization. The educators often tried to influence the brightest of the students to study the respective educators' specialization. In the first two years the teacher educators were seldom amongst those who taught mathematics or physics. They had little chance to keep pace in this respect with those who taught these subjects, and therefore, to recruit the students capable, as well as enthusiastic enough, to be mathematics teachers. These circumstances only helped to lower the status of teacher education. The conviction that the student who failed in the discipline specializations could prosper in teacher education was not admitted openly by all educators, but it nevertheless proved itself correct in too many cases to be taken for a mere prejudice. The policy of the "common first two years" served only seemingly well to the development of students in the fields of mathematics (or physics) as a science. It is commonplace that poor teachers are seldom successful in educating students to become well prepared, and for stimulating them to be eager enough to study science.

Dissatisfied teacher educators were fighting for many years to persuade the academicians to abandon the "common first two years" principle. The situation changed in 1967, when the program of the teacher study started to alter gradually. From 1968, there were separate lectures in mathematics (and physics) for students who wanted to be mathematicians, physicists or teachers. The courses of psychology, pedagogy, and didactics of mathematics were distributed evenly over all five years of the program of teacher study. Better linkage of these subjects was accomplished and, as the consequence of it, students' better readiness for their practical training in schools was reached.

The discussion over the "common first two years" principle arose at our faculty again, after the velvet revolution. Supporters of that principle argued that the best teachers of mathematics graduated in the prewar period, when teacher education

55

was almost identical with the education of the mathematical specialists, a fact which nobody can deny. Another fact that also can not be denied is that it was a very rare case, that the graduate mathematician of that time actually did something other than teaching at school. As a matter-of-fact, all university students of mathematics were potential mathematics teachers and almost all their educators were former secondary school teachers of mathematics.

After the second world war, many new professions have appeared for which a high standard of a mathematical knowledge is indispensable. Many of these professions are very attractive by their very nature, some of them offer a much better life standard than could be attained in the teacher profession. Because of this, not all the brightest students want to become mathematics teachers. The goal of mathematics teacher education is to make good teachers of the majority of those who expressed their willingness to be the ones by starting these courses--another reason for the special approach to their mathematical education.

The research work in the mathematics teacher education and in didactics of mathematics is not an easy work to do besides being seldom appreciated by the researchers in the exact sciences like mathematics. I do not believe that the things will change much in this respect for some years to come. I am convinced though that there are growing number of problems in teaching science, mathematics in particular, for the research of which methods should be developed and solutions of which found by the people capable to intermediate between the particular natural science and social sciences.

How I Became A Teacher Educator

Spæt Henriksen
Denmark

I would like to base the story of my life on the following question: Who am I? How did I become the one I am and what is essential and valuable in life--all from the perspective of my work with pedagogics.

My name is Elisabeth Spæt Henriksen. I suppose that I am the only person called Spæt, which is a kind of abbreviation of Elisabeth. Avoiding common abbreviations such as Lis, Beth, or Lisbeth, my parents preferred to create a new version. They also broke the tradition of wanting the firstborn to be a boy. But at the same time my life was characterised by the fact that a girl should be equal to a boy when it came to education. It had a decisive impact on my life for geographical reasons.

I was born in 1926 in Asiat in Greenland by Danish parents. In 1925, my father went to Greenland as the only Danish teacher in the country. Greenland became his whole life, he established the educational system from scratch and ended his career as Minister for Greenland.

There was no school for Danish children back then, so my schooling was put together in different ways. The elementary knowledge I learned from a private teacher. Some subjects I took at a Greenland school. I spoke the language fluently. But most of the time I taught myself. I read an incredible amount of difficult books

57

which I now find myself re-reading with wonder. What did I get out of them back then?

In 1938, I was sent back to Denmark to attend a proper school. There was a wide worry among Danish parents that the children should become too "Greenland," so when they were 12 years they had to return to the motherland. It was the intention that my parents should join me the next year, but then the Second World War broke out. I did not see them until 1945.

My two siblings were sent to the U.S.A. to attend school.

It was a shock to me to meet another culture. As the ship sailed down the Sound in the month of July I discovered an intense scent of country. It was impossible for me to identify it, but someone told me that it was the scent of trees. I was used to a scentless nature in a polar country.

I was also astonished by the size of the kale at the shore. It turned out to be trees. But I had never seen a tree; kale I knew. It took me many years to get used to trees; they obstructed the view.

Later I could use this knowledge in my work with formation of language and ideas.

The encounter with a real school was a big and frightening experience. I did not understand what went on. I did not know the rules. But I was deeply fascinated by everything I was to learn.

The headmaster wrote to my father that I was a sweet girl but had problems following the class. To encourage me, my father sent me a book with the dedication to his clever girl.

Much to the surprise of my teachers I passed the exam at the end of the year with brilliance. Neither I nor my classmates were surprised, for my classmates had instructed me how to behave like a good pupil. They recommended that I sit up front, looked interested, tried to get eye contact with the teacher and put up my hand, also when I did not know the answer. I learned it almost too well.

Later these experiences have also helped me understand why some children manage better than others.

The hidden curriculum is not always hidden for the pupils but properly for the teachers.

In 1945, I graduated and returned to Greenland and as my father lacked teachers at the continuation school I taught some Danish children there in my spare time.

But what should I train as? Preferably I would have liked to study literature at the University, but my father's finances could not manage that and I was not so independent as to manage by myself. It ended with my entering N. Zahle´s Teacher Training College for Women in 1946. I did not like it as I would have preferred something else.

I graduated as a teacher in 1950 and at the same time I had married and had the first child after ten months of marriage. Despite this the training college discussed whether I should be allowed to finish my education. They argued that it would be best for the child if I cared for it. I was the married student and I guess the first as well.

In 1998, at the time of writing this, my marriage is still surviving and the child is doing fine.

I was employed as a teacher in Gladsaxe, a suburb to Copenhagen, in 1950. Gladsaxe was a municipality in development with new comers from the most strained neighbourhoods of Copenhagen.

As the new teacher I was given the responsibility of a class of children from such a neighbourhood. It was a tough encounter with reality which a nice girl such as I knew nothing about. Among the pupils was a tired girl who had looked after her baby brother all night while her mother was working nights as a prostitute. I thought the girl was lazy. Everything I had learned at the most prestigious training college for girls was worth nothing.

After two years and more children I gave up and took care of my own. Back then there were only public day care for those of limited means.

At the same time I sometimes taught at the first little school, a progressive school whose pedagogic ideas were inspired by Dewey among others.

These years became decisive for my future life.

In 1962, I has employed at Ingrid Jespersen´s School, where the elementary introduction was inspired by progressive international pedagogics.

In 1964, I returned to Gladsaxe and was involved in developing a new pedagogic practice in order to follow up on the new Education Act from 1958.

From 1966 to 1967, I was back at the little school to get freer work space to develop the children centred activity pedagogics which I had as an ideal.

In 1967 I was encouraged to apply for a post at a teacher training college. It was important now to train teachers who could administer the new Education Act.

At the same time I studied pedagogics at the Royal Danish School of Educational Studies (RDES). In 1974 I got a master's degree in pedagogics. Again I was tempted to change my workplace, even though I was glad to be where I was.

I was a lecturer in pedagogics at RDES from 1974 to 1996. Afterwards I became a senior employee at the same place as well as a teacher of adult pedagogics at the Open University at Roskilde University Centre.

As a lecturer I have in particular worked with action research in primary education and taught candidates in pedagogics.

It is the progressive pedagogics which has occupied me: to understand it, develop it, evaluate it in a critical cultural perspective which have lead me into society theory.

My main focus has been to develop theory and practice so that the learners, children as well as adults, can get much more understanding of their own learning process and at the same time acquire the knowledge, insight and competence to act responsibly in their communities. I also encourage my students to acquire competence to consider critically what is going on and act on it.

A Personal Account of Education and Teacher Training in England 1921-1978

Kathleen E. Manning
England

Personal Education

In 1921 I went to a kindergarten class at age 3 in a very small church school in London, where I stayed until I was 5 years old. I transferred then to a larger school for children of ages 5-14. I was in the infant department, which was called a "mixed" department for boys and girls. When I was 7, in 1925, my family moved to Lancashire and there I went to school in Salford, which is adjacent to Manchester, a very poor town with many slum areas. There I went to a school similar to my school in London, with an infant department for boys and girls aged 5-7, a department for girls aged 7-14 and a separate department for boys aged 7-14. It was a three story building with the infants on the ground floor, the "big girls," as they were called, on the floor above and the boys on the top floor. There was a Head Teacher for each department. Some male teachers were employed in the "big boys" department and the Head Teacher of this department was male, all other teachers were female and unmarried. I stayed at this school until I was 11 years old when I passed a scholarship examination to go to another school which was called a grammar or high school. If my parents had been able to afford for me to go to a school of this standard, they could have paid fees, but my father was a policeman and didn't earn sufficient money, so I could only go to this school by passing a scholarship examination which meant my fees were paid by the state. I stayed at this girls school until I was 18 years

61

old and was in the same class as girls who were fee paying. In some ways the girls who were fee paying were treated with more consideration than the few girls, who like myself, were scholarship girls.

Ninety pupils were admitted to this school each year and were divided into three classes or "forms," with 30 girls in each form. After the first year we were graded according to ability. The most able girls were allowed to study Latin and French, the next able girls studied German and French, the least able girls studied only one language, namely French. If a pupil was in the A stream, which was the Latin form, she had a slightly different curriculum from the other forms. For example, in the A form, pupils studied subjects that were considered academic such as physics and chemistry, no domestic economy and very little art. The girls who were in the lowest class studied sewing, domestic economy, art and music in addition to basic academic subjects. I studied history, Latin, French, English language, English literature, geography and mathematics, which was divided into three sections: arithmetic, algebra and geometry. We had very little music and no art. All pupils had physical education sessions and games. There was one games afternoon a week and also on Saturday morning. In winter we played hockey and netball, in summer we played tennis, cricket and rounders--a form of baseball. There was a school uniform that everyone was required to wear. School rules were strict; for example, if a pupil was seen outside school not wearing gloves and the regulation uniform and badge by one of the teachers or a member of the public, she was taken to the head mistress and severely reprimanded.

There were school examinations at Christmas and in the summer, and at the end of the fifth year the first external examination. This examination was called Matriculation, with a lower level called School Certificate. The German and Latin classes entered for Matriculation, the other class entered for School Certificate. It was necessary to pass a certain combination of subjects to receive Matriculation. In my day a student could only take this once and it had to be taken at the age of 16. If a student gained the Matriculation Certificate, she could remain at school until the age of 18, if she failed she was required to leave at 16.

Between the years from Matriculation Certificate to the next public examination which was called a Higher School Certificate, a student was in the sixth form and was required to select the subjects which she wanted to continue to study. If she wished to go to university she selected those subjects in which she would gain entrance to the university course of her choice, but the school decided who would take university entrance exams. If she did not gain entrance to university and wished to continue her education she applied to enter a college. At that time there were very few careers for academically inclined girls other than teacher training.

As a small child I had wanted to teach because I liked young children. As I wanted to continue my education, and was presumed clever, the only avenue open for me was teacher training. University teacher training required first a degree and then a year's training for a diploma. There was no first degree in education; students had to get a degree in another subject and then continue with teacher training.

On leaving school at 18 in 1937, I passed an examination and gained entrance to the four year graduate teacher training course at Manchester University. I took a Bachelor of Arts Degree with honours in history. As an honours student accepted by the Education Department for teacher training, my fees were paid all through my university studies. It was difficult to get into teacher training at university level. At that time, a teacher was considered qualified to teach without teacher training and without a teaching certificate; therefore, a graduate trained as a teacher was a rarity. I took my honours degree and at the end of three years entered the Education Department at Manchester University. In 1937 Manchester University was the only university in Europe that trained graduate teachers to teach young children. There were only six students in my year training to teach children from the age of 3-11. Within that age range a student could opt for nursery (ages 3-5), infants (ages 5-7) or junior (ages 7-11). I opted to teach as a specialized teacher in the infant age range. Although I covered the whole range from 3-11, the age group I was most interested in was from 3-7. I chose this range because there was the scope to be creative as there were no examinations nor prescribed curriculum, except the basic skills, in Infant Schools.

The training I received in the education department at Manchester University was very progressive, but purely academic. There was little practical training to prepare teachers for the classroom. In one year I had three periods of practicum, or "school practice," in nursery, infant and junior schools in the Manchester inner city area. There were at least fifty children in a class and I received very little supervision and no practical help. It was difficult because the kind of teacher training in the university was modern and not in keeping with the practice of the teachers in the schools. I tried to devise ways in which I could put theory into practice in classroom

63

situations, but teachers weren't in sympathy and even if they could have helped wouldn't have wished to do so because they resented graduates coming into primary schools. Much of the theory we received introduced us to Piaget who at that time was becoming known in English education circles, but regarded with suspicion by practising teachers.

At the end of my year's training, I received an education diploma from the university which qualified me to teach children aged 3-11. If I had not passed the examination sufficiently highly to receive a diploma from the university, I would automatically have received a teacher training certificate from the government. This was the qualification that two year trained students received in teacher training colleges. However, because I was a graduate, I also received my teacher's certificate and two extra increments in salary as recognition for two extra years education. From 1941 to 1947 I taught in three primary schools in inner city areas and was then appointed as head teacher of an infant school in a suburban area. Women teachers received less salary than men and primary teachers less than secondary teachers.

Professional Educator in Teacher Training

During World War II children had been taught by male teachers who were too old to be conscripted into the armed forces or war work. The existing colleges were too small and few to train the requisite number of new teachers. In 1947 the government, therefore, instituted intensive one year "emergency" teacher training courses for mature ex-service men and women in residential colleges in disused army and navy camps.

A new Education Act in 1944 ruled that all teachers must be certificated. Those who had taught uncertificated for more than twenty years received automatic certification. Special one year training courses were established in existing colleges for teachers who had taught uncertificated for less than twenty years. The majority of these were women infant teachers working in rural schools. Cheshire Teacher Training College was one of the colleges chosen by the Government to conduct such a course. Cheshire Education Authority appointed me as a Lecturer in this college, where I organised a one year training course for emergency trained infant and junior teachers and a specialist course for the uncertificated infant teachers. The Ministry of Education approved both courses despite the fact that I had only eight years practical experience in schools, and none in teacher training colleges.

The principal of Cheshire Teacher Training College which was affiliated with Liverpool University applied to the university for approval to supersede the recognised examination by a system of continuous assessment. This was an innovation in teacher training at that time and an interesting experiment in which to be involved. Prior to the war most teacher training colleges had been one sex, residential and relatively small. Cheshire Teachers College had 400 men and women students and was at that time one of the larger colleges. The 1944 Education Act reduced class size and reorganised schools and a post war "baby boom" increased the school population. Many new large training colleges were built. University education faculties expanded and consequently the focus of teacher training changed. Courses that had been almost entirely practical embraced more theory and "education" and included more components--e.g. sociology, philosophy, psychology. Initially senior lectureships, later principal lectureships and eventually heads of departments were appointed, prior to this all teacher training college lecturers had been at the same rank and salary scale. Teacher training colleges incorporated further education for their 18 year old students who were required to study two subjects in addition to education. Those training to teach older pupils studied the subjects they would teach.

In 1959, after ten years in Cheshire Training College I was invited to apply for a post in the Education Faculty at Manchester University to train graduate primary teachers. As I had become accustomed to two year training and extended school practice periods I found the short university year and brief practice periods unsatisfactory. Two years later I accepted a post at the Margaret McMillan Memorial Training College in Bradford, Yorkshire. Teacher Training Colleges had now become Colleges of Education providing three year courses rather than two year courses. I worked in a continuous assessment form of evaluation, such as I had used at Cheshire College. Bradford was one of the first cities in England to support a large East Indian immigrant population. The schools and college were engaged in trying to resolve the problems raised by children from non-English speaking families, and this was my inauguration to adapting courses that would prepare teachers for changing situations in inner city schools.

In 1961 my next college was in Brighton in the south of England--a large highly academic college for men and women training to teach in primary and secondary schools. In 1968 the government ruled that the teaching profession should be an entirely graduate profession and that colleges of education (which had always been affiliated to universities) should be permitted to institute a first degree in education. Brighton, being an academically focused college affiliated to Sussex University, established an honours Bachelor of Education Degree which initially took four years.

During twenty five years, 1949-1974, in teacher training colleges and colleges of education I witnessed a change from one year courses for uncertificated teachers to two, then three year courses for non-graduate teachers and finally four year courses for an all graduate professional teaching qualification. Many teachers who had not been able to become graduates in college were able to continue teaching and obtain a first degree in dducation through the Open University. A first degree in Education, the B.Ed., Bachelor in Education, had been accepted.

Mature students with special training or experience had qualified for condensed teacher training courses in selected colleges throughout the country, for example, Bradford and Brighton. Inservice training for teachers was minimal when I entered the teaching profession. Specialist associations such as the Nursery Schools' Association would arrange summer schools or weekend seminars that teachers paid to attend in their free time. The Ministry of Education organised an annual one week summer school which was always over subscribed. University extra-mural departments realised the lack of inservice training and began to organise specialist evening courses extending over one, two or three terms, staffed by College of Education lecturers. I was involved in such work through Liverpool, Manchester, Leeds, London, and Sussex Universities and came to value the influence of inservice education in schools. Education Authority Advisers had increased in number and collaborated with college staff in the provision of inservice training.

The inservice work I had done alerted me to the need for teachers to examine the "play curriculum" in infant schools and evaluate its educational content. A grant from the government and local education authorities enabled a colleague and me to engage in action research with a group of 600 teachers in 200 schools for three years. A subsequent fourth year grant was used to establish workshops for teachers who had not been involved in the original project. This work reinforced my conviction that inservice training is an important part of the process of teacher training--the development of a highly qualified profession.

Resulting from the action research and the training materials produced (i.e. videotapes, books, and workshop courses) I conducted summer schools throughout the United Kingdom and Canada after I retired in 1978.

From 1921 to 1998 I have been involved in many changes in education in my country--as a pupil, teacher, and teacher educator. I have seen many small rural and infant schools close, and some infant schools combined with junior schools, which I believe it detrimental to the education of young children. Compulsory schooling has been raised from 14 to 16 years of age, and further education became free for all. Universities increased in number, teaching became a graduate profession, men and women received equal salaries, there were more professions opened to women, and more mixed sex schools and colleges.

Now I see the wheel turning--fees are reintroduced for further education students and university courses, differential salaries suggested for "high-flying" teachers, single sex schools increased in number, and private education becomes more popular.

There will always be changes and I know I will not necessarily agree with them all, but I also know I will never stop believing in education and fighting for my beliefs. I have never regretted becoming a teacher.

Teacher Education: A Mission for Equality Among Students

Margareth Drakenberg
Finland

Teacher education is a challenging but also rewarding career option. It Is a profession I gradually have grown into--not something I always have opted for.

I was born in 1943 in a small country-side community, Vintrosa, in Sweden and I remember my elementary school years as happy and generating all-round development. This school was characterized by having only two classrooms and a very restricted number of students in each grade. One room captured grades 1 and 2, while we in the other room would find grades 3 to 7. The teachers were lovely and we pupils felt these country-side teachers really understood us and helped us in growing into adults. In this classroom setting I learnt in particular to focus on what I was doing--but also, occasionally, to listen in what was going on in higher grades.

At the age of 13 I had to transfer to another school in a nearby city in order to continue my education. This transfer was a cultural chock although I did not understand it that way while it was in progress. The change of school meant extremely long school-days due to the geographical distance between my home and the school and even the very timetable for the buses. The culture in this city-school involved dress-changes every lunch break, and students who, for different reasons, could not stand up to this custom were definitely unpopular. However, what surprised most of all were the prejudices the teachers of this school had towards country-side students. We were expected to know nothing and to understand even less. And I think it was during these school-years, up to "realexamen" (comparable today to diploma from junior high school), that I made up my mind that if I would survive this very hostile treatment, so devastating to my self-confidence, I would try to become a teacher myself and via an understanding and caring behaviour help also students from the country-side to get on well in higher education schools.

As you can see I survived these years of upheaval and since then, an outsider would say, I have gone from strength to strength. In 1964 I qualified for entrance to the university in order to become a secondary school teacher in the Swedish language and literature, and history. Having finished my language studies I turned to history and encountered the most boring teacher I have ever seen, so I quickly changed to the studies of pedagogy needed for the teacher certificate.

Studying education gave me answers to many of my own questions about school, school culture, teaching and learning. So instead of studying history I changed my direction and focused on more pedagogy, and psychology. In 1971 I graduated and the following year, after having given birth to our second son, I continued to post-graduate studies. By now I had completely forgotten about my promise to myself to become a teacher because the studies in education were so interesting and rewarding. In 1978 I presented and defended my Ph.D.-thesis about "Continuity in change in the mental performance process. A longitudinal study of 10-13 year old children." That year I was granted a post-doctoral scholarship and honored as Honorary Fellow at the department of curriculum and instruction at the University of Wisconsin, Madison. Here I was given the opportunity to deepen my knowledge and experiences of school-childrens' thinking and understanding in mathematics, as well as my experiences of the longitudinal research method.

In December 1979, after 18 months in United States, I and my family returned to Sweden and I was offered an appointment as a teacher educator at a teacher education college about 300 kilometers from where my family was living. I felt it strange to be a teacher educator, never having been a teacher. All of a sudden, having the formal education needed, a Ph.D., I was qualified as a teacher educator and qualified to tell others how to teach--something I had never done myself! In such a situation good advice is expensive, so friendly and nice teacher educators at that teacher college taught me to be a teacher educator. I will never forget those lessons, they have helped me along hundreds of times, so also for the future. Some tough but wonderful years passed as I grew as a teacher, as a teacher educator and as a person.

70

But it was difficult to have my small own school-children at one place and myself at another so after some years, when an opportunity was given I was appointed university lecturer in the town where my family was living. This appointment involved full-time teaching, and my teaching duties were, due to the departmental policy, restricted to the pre-graduate level. Graduate level and supervision were duties for men, only. I stayed for too many years, but no other appointment was available and increases or changes in my responsibilities were out of question. Advancement was considered a man's privilege!

In 1991 I was given the opportunity to move to University of Helsinki in Finland and almost immediately was appointed a position as associate professor. Here I am given frequent opportunities to grow, to increase my knowledge and understanding of pedagogical issues and to work according to my interests and capability. As associate professor I am involved in full-time teaching and on top of that--and not officially included in the appointment--I am supervising as well as doing research for publication. The strange thing is, however, that supervision, research, administration, and coordinating activities with other universities are expected but not paid. On top of the teaching duties, it means that weekends and holidays often have to be used to squeeze in time for supervision and my own research activities. In spite of that and, sometimes, language problems, I like being at University of Helsinki. I am again a teacher educator, a career I find very challenging.

My tough years as a school kid have long since passed and school has changed. Still, there are differences in treatment--not due to geographical or economical reasons but due to creed, colour, customs, or race. So far, I have in Helsinki been given the possibilities to work according to my capacity and beliefs of equality and I hope that I will be given the chances to continue on my way to attain equality among students.

The faculty of Education at the University of Helsinki is the largest faculty of its kind in Finland. The faculty supports 130 teachers and researchers and houses about 2200 students. Also students from other faculties are studying at the faculty of education in order to become subject teachers.

There are presently only two departments at the faculty: Department of Teacher Education and the Department of Education. The latter is historically the first, founded in 1955. This department is bilingual, and it is possible to study education and adult education in Swedish as well as Finnish. The Swedish speaking students are studying at this department to become teachers because education at the Department of Teacher Education is in Finnish. At the Department of Education, students are offered degrees of different kinds, from graduation to the doctoral degree. I am working within the Swedish speaking section and my responsibilities are, first of all, full-time teaching. On top of that I am supervising a number of students at graduate and post-graduate levels, I am doing research for publication, cooperating with researchers in other countries, responsible for cooperation and coordination with some other universities, involved in curriculum development and responsible for parts of the Open University's courses and degrees in education.

Worldwide interdependence and globalisation are major forces in contemporary private and professional life. So since the 1960s, the whole field of education has in Sweden been subject to far-reaching organisational reforms. These changes have in many different ways influenced teachers' professional and private lives. Current topics in teacher discussions and debates are: teachers' accountability, career possibilities, changing roles and culture in schools- more violence today than ever before. As a consequence I think the future challenges will be about the quality of education, the relationship between educational research and teachers' professional development, and finally about finding time and a place for teachers to discuss and reflect upon their own knowledge and experiences.

In confronting the many challenges that the future holds in store, I see education an indispensable asset in its attempt to attain moral and social responsibility enacted through curriculum, pedagogy, interpersonal relationship and classroom management.

My Story

Karlheinz Rebel
Germany

When starting to write my story I was puzzled how to really build in a structure into life's (seemingly) chaotic sequence of unconnected events. But on second thought and using the request to write the story of my becoming an educator as a challenge there I really found something which ran like a thread through all these puzzling events and happenings since I was born in 1923.

To a certain extent the school career in Germany until today very much decides which options are open to a youngster. During my career as a pupil and student in the thirties this was even much more the case than today. So, all those who show a certain ambition and seem intellectually gifted enough--at least in their parents' eyes--used to go to the so-called 'Gymnasium,' similar to the old type of the English grammar school, with the almost only aim to become mature for studying at a German university, i.e., to organize their studies by themselves without very much support from the university staff's side. When a student, after 13 years of schooling, of these nine years in a gymnasium, earns the final Gymnasium certificate, the 'Abitur,' he or she is entitled to study at any German university any subject he or she wants to, provided the university capacity in the faculty in question is sufficient (which has to be proved if a student is refused matriculation and goes to the Courts). When I attended this type of school between 1934 and 1941 it was extremely selective, as only about 4-5% of those born in one year went there, and by far, not all of them reached the final grade 9 or passed the final exam. Studies were almost exclusively oriented at the acquisition of academic knowledge: for example, a perfect style in German if possible, influenced by the Latin, Greek, and German classics; at least perfect spelling; Latin from the very first to the 9th grade; the same with mathematics; from the third grade on a modern second language (in the old languages department it used to be French); and from the fourth grade on, old Greek. In addition pupils studied history, geography, two or three sciences, drawing, and music. As a whole we used to have something like 12 subjects, most of them from grade 1 to grade 9 of the gymnasium, and most of them examined in the 'Abitur.' The pedagogic maxim for this rather rigid approach with its comprising curriculum was primarily called 'general breeding'. The educators of that era were convinced that this type of study constituted the optimal basis for any later profession-oriented education and training at a university, with a high transfer potential. The old languages and mathematics were especially thought to enable the students to learn how to think logically. Learning modern languages was done by especially learning the Latin grammar structure in this foreign language; knowing the grammar of it including the numerous variations from the rules a sufficiently broad vocabulary basis, and most important--the ability to translate from one's own into the foreign language or the other way round. I had French for six years, but we never made conversation in the foreign language. As a consequence I am still able to apply some grammar rules to and get the meaning of a text passively, but I cannot converse with French people. The very first live French exemplars I met was when I happened to run into a group of French prisoners of war and tried to make a little conversation with them (which was of course strictly forbidden, but curiosity...). My frustration was high when I realized that I could not communicate with them. For the first time in my life I had serious doubts about the adequacy of such methodic approaches.

But let's go back to my first steps after the primary school. When I had reached the age of 11 it was high time to go to the nearest gymnasium, but this was about 25 kilometres away from my place which meant--quite contrary to today's conditions--daily commuting and extensive hours of waiting at the station (rooms in my school where we could have stayed during the waiting hours, perhaps doing our homework after school had finished did not exist). So I was either exhausted after being back home or had lost any interest in what had been going on in school, with the consequence that I inevitably got on the losers' list. Usually I did homework in the train between school, city and home or home and place of school, or to be more accurate, I relied heavily on the work of my schoolmates and copied what they had already done at home because their parents had an eye on them. Before I totally failed in this gymnasium and became a hopeless case having to go back into the 'Volksschule' (providing elementary and secondary education for the majority of youngsters not aiming at an academic career) which was then considered as something to be ashamed of, my father took me to a private Catholic boarding school about 50-60 kilometres from home, known for maintaining a strict working discipline, but also offering much promotion for the individual student (quite unusual in the then German public gymnasium with its educational principle: 'Like it or lump it!'). This meant for my father a rather risky decision because he, as a civil servant in the Nazi regime, was not allowed to support the church schools. Several times he was summoned to his senior officers and unpleasantly questioned about the reasons for his insubordination. He was certainly not politically educated and probably did not see what it was really all about. But he instinctively despised the Nazis he personally happened to know and mistrusted their promises. For example, when I, as a seven year old kid, told at the family table a primitive joke about Charlemagne I had heard from some Nazi youngster, he gave me my first political box on the ear which was quite impressive (the second followed two years later when I told a similarly ugly joke about Hindenburg, the President of the German Reich; only that this time my school teacher applied it to me!). My father continued to feel suspicious of the Nazis, and although he expected consequences, nothing serious happened to him. Judging by today's knowledge of the working of the Nazi regime this was not unusual in the middle of the thirties, because the main aim of the regime in its first years was to create an atmosphere of uncertainty and fear. Most people fell into this trap, too often practising a kind of anticipating obedience to the regime. This changed only when the WW II broke out in 1939. At that time the whole daily brutality of this regime came out also in the public.

For me, my father's decision was the most important event in my biography; I not only within a few months caught up with the others in my class, but much more importantly, I was deeply influenced by quite a number of knowledgeable, enthusiastic teachers, one of them--a Catholic priest and a genius in mathematics and the old languages including Hebrew--became my 'spiritual father' who during the whole War tried to help me, to encourage me to live the value pattern he and some others had implanted in me. The boarding school belonged to the Archbishop of

Freiburg, and so it was the main aim of the Nazi Party to make out of it a so-called 'Napola,' a Nazi school for their cadres, and it was the main aim of the Archbishop and those in the staff who were against the Nazis to prevent the other side from doing so. My 'father in spirit' also encouraged my friends and me to disturb the Nazi plans as much as we could. And so we did. Our school remained intact till the end of the War, but our group made incredible mistakes, being naive and totally unpolitical. The secret police searched our cupboards after we had come back from a summer camp, questioned us and threatened to institute a court procedure which could have meant concentration camp and the end of my school career. In this situation the Archbishop intervened. The oldest in our group were sent to a 'trustworthy' unit of the German Army (I was not yet 18 years old), and the Gestapo files disappeared.

All the time I was in this school I did not think of becoming an educator. I had started learning to play the violin at the age of six, and I was then determined to become a second Paganini. But I had also developed a rather wide scope of interests being a product of our German general breeding philosophy. For example, I admired great engineers and their work. I was eager in experimenting with chemicals and I devoured books, especially novels. When I, during the questioning by the Gestapo, was asked about my future plans, I mentioned the violin and the engineering as my favourites. The former did not interest them much, but the latter was the cause that I was sent to an armoured division becoming first a tank driver. Later I became lieutenant. I took part in military actions in the Caucasian war theatre, then belonged to the German Army which was ordered to break up the Russian blockade of Stalingrad and free the enclosed German troops (the attempt failed). I was on the long retreat over thousands of kilometres via the Don, the Ukraine, Romania, Poland, and finally the then Czechoslovakia. I was wounded three times, the last time by American troops in Germany, and became a prisoner of war, being for about three quarters of a year in a military hospital in Fulda. When still in Russia I realized that I had to give up my dreams of becoming a violinist; the interruption by the war and injuries at my shoulder made such a career impossible. Therefore I applied to Karlsruhe Technical University as a chemistry student. I was sent study material even to Russia as long as the military postal services were functioning. In the war hospital I learned about the American Morgenthau Plan. My conclusion from this was that chemistry in Germany had no real chance in the future of the country. I felt rather despaired, but exactly at this time I got a message from my 'spiritual father' who had managed to reach me, even as a prisoner of war. through the All-German Bishop's Conference which used to have its meetings in Fulda. Without knowing of my plight he suggested to me to become a teacher and come to him as soon as possible. He argued that in such times teachers are much more important than almost any other profession to help to heal the intellects and the minds of the young people. He wrote me also in his function as principal of the boarding school I had attended. I became convinced by him, and after dismissal from the hospital, I started my studies at Heidelberg University. I had chosen German literature, history and politics, and English (which I never had at school; but I wanted a modern foreign language, and I could not take French as the leading professors of German and French fought each other and had their main lectures exactly on the same time.) Again I seemed to have tried to escape the real challenge of the teaching profession, and the German system made it easy for me not to think of my future job as a teacher. I enjoyed my subject field studies; we students were like dried out sponges drawing in what could help us to reorient ourselves and to become current with international developments. Only English was a crux, but gradually by reading English novels (*Tom Jones* was my first English reading), listening to BBC language programmes (the university at that time did not offer language courses but concentrated on the philological aspects offering lectures and seminars on important, influential figures of literature, literary periods, history of language etc.), and finding a girl friend (my wife now) who excelled in English pronunciation and polished mine up! I managed to pass the English exam. If I had been the examiner this would not have happened!

Before I could start the induction period in a gymnasium in Heidelberg, my 'spiritual father' intervened again, and he managed to get permission to be my personal tutor and prepare me for the second state exam to become a fully fledged gymnasia teacher. Everything went wonderfully. Teaching proved to be something I had not yet received a special training for, but it allowed me to identify myself with my work, and my students were grateful for this engagement. My first class of English in grade nine had many more years of English studies than I had. But they instinctively wanted more than just an expert in Anglistics, and I could give them at least partly what they wanted. I quickly made a career, became responsible for the English Department, managed to have permanently a young student from a British university working with us for one year, the first in a German school. But soon I realized that enthusiasm and involvement are not enough to fully use the potential given to us by our schools. I started to study literature on education, didactics, methods, and media. Teachers from several gymnasium of our region constituted a working group. We discussed new pedagogic literature, visited each other in our lessons, arranged festivals, theatre visits and dozens of other activities. I liked teaching more and more, enjoyed interacting with my students, and I gradually realized how little I knew. Of course, I had wonderful help from the principal and friend. He probably wanted me to become his successor. And I learned to distinguish between his care for me, and the necessity to find my own way. My experiences as a gymnasium teacher, as trainer of student teachers, and my activities in educational television and radio programmes, but also my many travelings abroad made me aware that, on the one hand, working with youngsters and later with university students as a teacher was a job I liked to do and could do well. But, on the other hand, I had to realize how quickly I had become a 'Routinier,' meaning that I was increasingly relying on routines, without being able to use what potential good theories can offer us. I managed my teaching and education tasks. My students, most of my colleagues, and the parents were satisfied, but I became more and more dissatisfied. I felt that I was kept prisoner of my success and my career.

But before I gave up hope and became 'satisfied' almost at the same time I received two offers which changed my whole situation. I was offered the position of principal of a new gymnasium which included a boarding home. I worked there for two years, 1964 and 1965. A little earlier I was offered a lecturer position at Hamburg University and the Free University Berlin allowing me to study a second time after 15 years of teaching in the gymnasium. After some hesitation I took to the second offer from 1966 on. I decided to drop everything (most people who heard of my decision thought me totally crazy; and also my fellow lecturers, usually young assistants to a professor, did first not know how to approach me). I had qualified for my lectureship by my private studies which are quite unusual and should not be recommended to others for imitation: I used to intensify my private studies after a certain 'chapter' had been finished by writing papers, making television programmes on these topics etc. And so some people noticed me and gave me a chance at the university again. This step back to the university in the middle of the sixties was hard. At that time practice was considered by many educators at universities to spoil the pureness of theory; and pedagogy became in the understanding of many university educators 'science of education,' far from the 'lowly spheres' of practical work. The consequence on the practising teachers on the other hand was that they felt totally defeated, and found the culprit in theory. Some almost developed a kind of phobia against theoretical work, technical terms, etc.

For my second study period I chose science of education, psychology and sociology, and in 1975 received my doctorate in education, being all the time forced to earn my living. Mingled into these complicated changes was a third decisive turn in my life course. From 1967 on I was deputy director of a research institute on distance education, from 1979 on as director. But it had again to do with teacher education. My main working field was teacher inservice, and again I had to learn quite a number of lessons, not only in terms of research and scientific management, but also with regard to teacher education. In the last 30-40 years we certainly have had many important changes in this field in Germany. Practice has been invited to come back to my alma mater (we have now reached excellent standards, e.g. in teaching foreign languages), and many teacher educators try to find a synthesis between practice and theory, though we still have in Germany not enough of the practical aspects in our work. And we are still fighting to find a better balance between the subject field and the professional studies. This is still one of our weak points. Our students in most cases still have to find their own way through the labyrinth of lecture and seminar announcements for each semester, without a clear, sequenced curriculum in many subject field studies and in education. There is gradually a better awareness of these problems among some of our educational politicians which may prove to be an important step forward. But funny to say, many problems are exactly the old ones which sometimes had disturbed my sleep and had made me so restless.

When I look back, my career as an educator is absolutely atypical according to German measures. My long hard climb up to higher academic honors would have been impossible without the doctorate though it came rather late in my life. But I was spared the so called 'Habilitation,' the second doctorate to become professor at a university, by counting my publications as an equivalent. It also helped me to overcome the doubtful spots on my career which did not follow the 'oxen tour' from Abitur straightforward to the university, then after the diploma in education becoming 'scientific assistant' to the owner of an academic chair, then writing within another six or more years the 'Habilitation,' and then waiting for a call on one of the educational chairs. Probably at the age of about 40-45 a typical German will have

79

succeeded, totally academically socialized and being an expert in the theoretical framework of education, often on this long way forgetting the teachers! Only within the last few years this is slowly changing, and a new generation is gradually occupying the university chairs of education. So, there is hope even if it comes too late for me.

I should mention that I wrote this story solely under the perspective of the gymnasium, its teachers, and the teachers of the gymnasium teachers, the professors. Their difficulty is that education and professional studies as a whole do not count very much compared to the subject field studies which take our students at the moment about 12-14 semesters equals 6 to 7 years leaving only tiny little spots in their time-table where education may come in; not because people in this job like it very much or think it necessary, but mostly because it is demanded as a prerequisite for undergoing the ordeal of the first state examination in the subject field studies.

The preparation of the teachers of our primary and secondary one schools is very different from what I described. It is much more practice-oriented, but with the tendency to adapt to the university pattern to show its equality to the classical studies at a 'normal' university. But to discuss these other teacher careers would take the space for another story.

But I have to come back to my 'spiritual father.' He was such a wonderfully gifted teacher though without any pedagogical training, that he also became my 'pedagogic father.' My unorthodox way of studying and trying to make my career in teaching has meaning if I think of his way of educating his staff, and his students (he taught in students' classes his usual subjects in spite of his functions as director of a big and complicated school, knowing all his about 800 students by name; knowing of their problems and their family backgrounds). It was simply incredible when I watched him in his work. But he also had the gift to encourage me, his staff, to give us space to develop, to let us go when the time was ripe.

Meanwhile I am familiar with dozens of theories of educating, learning, structuring curricula, teaching methods, schools as systems, and the various controversial positions we have in Germany in the science of education. But during my professional work I have learned one lesson: without being able to be a good example to those we have to instruct and to educate, without identifying oneself with the teaching task, trying as much as is possible to meet the learner as a significant other, accepting, encouraging, helping, supporting him or her, these theories and academic models will not work. My 'spiritual and pedagogic father' taught me this lesson. And I was only successful and satisfied when I tried to follow this route, though imperfect as we all are or have to be to remain humble. But at the same time we all have to incorporate the theoretical equipment in order to be able to reflect what we are doing, to have a certain distance to our work, in spite of all enthusiasm. The combination of both: the example of an adored teacher educator and hard theoretical work seem to offer us one solution to the many problems we have to face in teacher education. At least this was and still is the thread in my professional life.

How I Became A Teacher Educator

Gabriella Gulyás
Hungary

I was born in 1954 and I have been teaching since 1979.

To become a teacher educator in Hungary there is a certain procedure to follow. One must take a five year course in a university to finish with an MA and as a secondary school teacher. There is then five year's teaching experience after finishing the degree before applying for a consulting teacher's job and to start a career as a teacher trainer. If a person is interested in this field, university methodologists visit the lessons to assess and evaluate the teacher's ability, then produce a report. They may recommend courses and further reapplication the following year, but those who are successful can qualify--no administration background is necessary.

However, I reached my position in a slightly different way. After five years of university study I gained my M.A. and found a job in a Technical College for Light Industry. I taught young aspiring engineering students English as part of their course--an extra part. I also had a part-time job at a university of economics teaching these students as well. I worked in these two jobs for ten years, with students who had no particular interest in what I was teaching them, and who had enough work from their own courses without mine in addition.

Disillusioned, I decided to take a teaching course to reawaken my interest. It was an ESP course which didn't do much for me in itself, but I met some colleagues there and we took part in a project that would change my job. I went back to my college and started a new teaching procedure. My classes worked together to produce a video series in a local textile factory. They filmed the factory at work and interviewed the employees. The video series was in English and provided a goal to work towards, and some relief from the students' heavy work load, as well as the technical content being a small help to their courses. In turn I used the completed series as a course book substitute in other classes--it was fully appreciated all around.

During this time a professor from the university approached me with an offer--to take a group of fifth year university students into my video classes to observe and then discuss afterwards. These students suddenly opened my mind to new ideas--they asked me questions I had never considered before, and I wanted to meet their demands.

The realisation hit me that after ten years in higher education I still had so much to learn. These students were actually challenging to talk to, they made me acutely aware of my lack of knowledge of methodology. But I really enjoyed these discussions--talking with bright students who were genuinely interested in what they were discussing, it stretched me but delighted me at the same time.

In 1991 the United States Information Service organised a course for teacher trainers. Lecturers from the U.S.A. came to speak and it was an excellent experience. Following this I applied for a consultant teacher job at Trefort Gimnázium where I also taught secondary school pupils. My application needed no visit from university methodologists because of the success of my video course. I was accepted and a year later was made deputy head of the school. This job involved being head of all language teaching in the school, international relations with other schools, organising trips abroad for the choir and so on--and also being head of the teacher training programme. Trefort is attached to the university and approximately two hundred students come each year for valuable teaching observation and practise. My job, like all the other consultant teachers in the school is to take on three students a year. We all have twelve lessons a week and our student teachers come to every one of these. There is a preclass discussion when we set the observation task, then the class which the student goes to, followed by a post observation discussion. After two to three weeks of this procedure the student starts teaching. After twenty lessons there is another period of observation by the student, during which they visit other students, classes and take part in their discussions. It helps for them to work together almost like a team--they can give a lot to each other from their own individual experiences.

The consultant teacher teaches only fourteen to eighteen year olds, with a trainee teacher from the fifth year in the university preparing to teach the same age group. We help and encourage our trainee teachers, using our experiences to help them, and prompting them into discovering the job themselves.

My job as deputy head, with all its other responsibilities limits the amount of consulting work I can actually do. Some consultant teachers also work part-time in Universities doing methodology seminars.

I feel the most important aspect of the training of teachers is empathy. A person has to have been there, and to understand the difficulties and joys of becoming a successful teacher. A teacher must help people to develop, and guide them into confidence. Too many consultants make the mistake of coming straight out with what was good and what was bad in a student's lesson. I remember in one course at the university a consultant who only criticised my lessons, instantly putting me on the defense. He 'dictated' to me what I should and shouldn't be doing--there was no equality or understanding; hence, I didn't learn anything from him, or respect him.

I love the company of young people. I became a teacher so I could always enjoy this. I get great satisfaction from teaching as well--watching my students learn and develop.

To me my trainee teachers are equals, they are, hopefully, going into a career of teaching for similar reasons, and therefore, I can feel some empathy towards them. In helping them to become better teachers I learn myself: this is most important, I feel. Many people say someone is born a good teacher but I disagree. Everyone can learn to become good at their job and the pursuit of this knowledge is a vital part of improvement. For me, my position today was not 'predestined.'

I try and encourage my students also to be aware of what they are doing in class, not to just go in and talk and then come out and forget what they said. I get them to repeat things they did in a lesson. This is difficult at first, but the more they practise the more lucid and clear their lessons become.

My experience is similar, if not exactly the same, as most consultant teachers in Hungary. At the moment, once teachers are appointed they can remain so for however long they wish. There is a movement, however, and I support it, which seeks to introduce another visit from university methodologists after five years, to see how the consultant is doing. Too many people get set in their job and refuse to change, which is dangerous. Teaching is a changing profession and always will be, which I suppose is part of the reason I am so interested in it.

Poets Are Born; Teachers Are Made
And Teacher Educators Are Moulded

Sneha Joshi
India

On September 22, 1943, an elite family in Bombay, India, celebrated the birth of a girl child. As an only child of the family, she was given the best of everything--undivided love, care, affection, and warmth of the family. At the same time, her parents were not over-protective (for that would not have helped her to grow into an independent, self-reliant person that she is today).

Yes, today she is the Dean of the Faculty of Education and Psychology, Head of the Department of Educational Administration, and Founder Secretary of Gujarat Council of Educational Administration (GCEA). She holds many more challenging positions and has earned a name for herself in the academic circles in India and abroad.

Well, it's me, Sneha Joshi, and I share my story of how I was moulded and groomed into what I am today.

Due to my father's frequent transfers, I had my early schooling in four different states. Apart from learning different languages and becoming familiar with various cultures of this vast country, I learnt to accept changes and even reckon them as challenges. It did pay a rich dividend in the long run. Yes, to a great extent, I was moulded by circumstances that came my way.

I recall with nostalgia those years that I was a student at St. Columba High School in Bombay. It was a home away from home. It was a boarding school exclusively for girls. The students had come from different parts of the country and we learnt to live in harmony in spite of the cultural differences.

We were trained and groomed to be self-reliant. The strict discipline, emphasis on self-study, systematic learning, sports, regular prayers, and active involvement in the various activities of the hostel have gone a long way in helping me understand the value of team-work and true leadership qualities.

After my graduation from the renowned Wilson College, Bombay, I married and for eight years I led my life as a contented housewife in a happy home with two lively children. I read a lot, but did not take up any serious academic pursuit.

In May 1972, I landed in Baroda, a city in the neighbouring state of Gujarat, with my seven year old son and three year old daughter, as my husband accepted a job in an industry based in Baroda. Because of my husband' encouragement, I entered the B.Ed. course in the Maharaja Sayajirao University of Baroda.

At this juncture I would like to mention that I opted for Educational Administration as my special subject. My request was turned down by the Admission Panel. The reason? "This subject is suitable for teachers with long years of experience, not for fresh entrants with no experience," they pointed out emphatically. Undaunted, I expressed my eagerness and convinced them to allow me to study the subject of my choice, namely, Educational Administration. but little did I realise that day what it would mean to me later in my life and my career.

My ambition, at that time, was to complete my B.Ed. and to take up a job in the same school where my children were studying. But Dr. M. B. Buch, Head of the Centre for Advanced Studies in Education, a centre with a unique national character and international reputation, encouraged me to pursue the M.Ed. degree. His immense faith in my potentials were instrumental in giving a new turn in my career.

I completed my M.Ed. degree with distinction and under the guidance of Dr. Buch, I completed my Ph.D. degree in 1977. Now I say it in one simple sentence, but the long hours of reading, stretching every hour into sixty worthy minutes, and with the endless hours of hard work and toil, I emerged as not just a Ph.D. Scholar, but an Educational Administrator with relentless enthusiasm and deep faith in the future of the nation.

I joined an English medium school as the Headmistress, but soon the academician in me wasn't very happy with the routine administrative work in a school.

I applied for the post of a Lecturer in Education as well as in Educational Administration and was selected for both. I opted for the latter and had to struggle to get due recognition in the institution. That was the time I solely devoted my energy, time, and enthusiasm for writing research papers and I participated in seminars, conferences, and discussions. Could I sit back complacent awaiting opportunities to roll down my way? No, I looked for them and fought for them. Whenever there were disappointments, hard work was the only antidote, and it yielded rich results.

I was appointed as a lecturer in the Department of Education in the Higher Education Unit in 1978. I was given the responsibility to organise inservice courses for the lecturers of M.S. University in methodology of teaching. I had to revise and recast the same course for several years. Each programme was revised and finally it took a good shape in orienting a new lecturer in his role as a lecturer in the university. I continued as the coordinator of the course until the time the University Grant Commission made the course compulsory for all the university lecturers when academic colleges were established.

In May 1987 I became a Reader in Education. One very important point I must add in this context is that, in the year 1986, I was not selected as a Reader in Educational Administration. That disappointment further motivated me and gave me good strength to prepare myself for a future career. I worked very hard and published more papers, took on research projects, tried to recruit Ph.D. students, and became the member of many professional associations in the country. Through these associations I came to know my eminent professors and scholars which brought me out of my institution into the academic world outside.

Simultaneously, I understood it was very important to work on administrative bodies in the university. I became an officer in the Baroda University Teachers Association and was elected to the Senate, the supreme authority of the university. I was the Vice President of BUTA (1987-1993). Once again in 1987, I appeared for an interview for the professor's post. No one was selected for this post, and in remained vacant. In the meanwhile, I was invited to work as a professor and Head and the Dean of the Faculty of Education, Bhavnagar University. I took one year's duty leave, and joined that university. During the year, I started a regular one year M.Ed. course which is considered to be a milestone in the development of that organisation. Also I revised the syllabus. I returned with success and a good reputation from that university. In 1990, I went to Britain for an International Intervisitation Programme as I thought learning about educational administration in other countries was very essential. That experience proved helpful. I then returned to my previous position.

Within six months, I was appointed as Professor and Head of Educational Administration in my university. This department had been started in 1951 but, after a few years, it deteriorated. All the courses were discontinued. The first thing I did was a training programme called Competency Based Institutional Management Education. This was reorganised at a national level from the Ministry of Human Resource Development, New Delhi. We trained all the school principals of Baroda. But real team work brought out successes to our department. This was an innovation which received recognition.

The success of the programme gave me courage to start a local under the umbrella of the Commonwealth Council of Education Administration. In April 1992, I visited Australia, Singapore University and universities in Bangkok as a visiting professor. In that year, we had also started a Professional Diploma in Educational Management with a good number of students. In 1993, I was invited as a visiting professor to the United Kingdom. I also visited UNESCO and the International Institute of Learning and Administration, both in Paris. I have made efforts to have collaborations with the above mentioned countries. I am sure we will be successful in building a network.

During my attendance at the International Seminar for Teacher Education in 1992, I came closer to teacher education in the United States, Canada, the United Kingdom, and Japan. College friends around the world are associated with me in a true sense of sending much literature on education and education administration. I am now on the Educational Advisory Committee for the Commonwealth Journal of Educational Administration.

These are some of the chapters of my success story. Whether it is the responsibility of being the syndicate member of M.S. University of Baroda or the committee member of All India Council of Technical Education (AICTE), government of India, or Programme Planning Committee of National Institute of Educational Planning and Administration (NIEPA), or International Association of Women Scientist, Italy, it is the positive approach that had helped me set my targets and work with involvement.

The Ph.D. theses I have guided and those in progress under my guidance cover a wide range of subjects and I have always taken up these as a mutual learning experiences. Whether it is a lecture on Educational Management or a routine schedule in an inservice training programme for school principals or conducting a viva voce examination for Ph.D./M.Ed., I believe in inspiring the students/candidates to think, to review, to analyse, and to deduce.

The success at my home front is an asset and a constant source of encouragement for me to strive on and on.

I believe in building institutions and encouraging institution builders. Over the years I have developed my own definition of leadership in the liberal sense. My success lies in building teams, identifying talents, and helping my younger colleagues find their own path of success.

The support and encouragement by all the members of my family and constant companionship of my husband have helped me a in my search for excellence. Now the Baroda Chapter of GCAE has brought us together as partners in a joint venture.

In 1998 I was awarded the Commonwealth Foundation Award by the Commonwealth Council of Education Administration and Management, United Kingdom. I have also been bestowed the honour of being the director of the programme for developing self-instructional modules on "Better School" for the training of school principals in India. This prestigious project is assigned by the Commonwealth Secretariat, London.

It has not always been a smooth ride. There have been set-backs, stumbling blocks, hardships, dead-ends, discouraging turns, disappointing moves, but I kept going, because I believe in doing and achieving.

I believe in living in actions not just in years. I wouldn't like my career to be measured in terms of the number of years of service, but by the deeds and the achievements.

Thus continues my story--it is an optimist's story of hard and dedicated work, enthusiasm, a positive outlook.

My Professional Growth as a Teacher Educator

Daniel N. Sifuna
Kenya

I was born on the 10th of May 1944 in Bungoma District of Western Province in a large family of nine boys and six girls. My father and mother were small scale farmers and petty traders. From early childhood, I had to participate in domestic chores especially assisting in farm work and herding cattle. Herding cattle was often quite exciting because it gave me the opportunity to socialize with children from other families during which we had make-shift plays which included wrestling, running, jumping, moulding toys, telling stories, and many others.

In our village during the late 1940s and early 1950s primary schools were very few. The nearest primary school was about 10 kilometers away. In 1951 when I was eight years old, my father decided to send me to a new primary school that was opening in the village roughly 4 kilometers from home. As motor vehicles and bicycles were generally few, I had to walk to school daily. The new school opened under a huge fig tree, which meant classes could not be held when it rained. Gradually, a temporary tuition block with several classrooms was erected by the community. Our seats consisted of stones or wooden logs. Teaching consisted of memorizing letters and words, written on the blackboard and often recited together with our teacher. In class one, or the first grade, we were initiated into writing by curving letters and words in the sand.

On graduating to Grade 2, my parents bought me a slate. Having been made of some hardened clay, it was a very fragile piece of material to maintain as it would break quite easily. The medium of instruction was in our mother tongue except in class four where English became the medium of instruction. By Grade 3, the community had improved the classroom facilities which included desks and the provision of exercise books. Text books were extremely rare, and only the class teacher possessed a copy. Discipline was rigidly maintained through caning with a stick.

In 1955, I sat for the Competitive Entrance Examination, a national examination taken in class four, to qualify for the few intermediate schools that existed in the country. Intermediate schools were advanced primary schools which had grades five to eight. The nearest intermediate school I was selected to join was boarding and was approximately 22 kilometers from home. As many of my brothers and sisters were now in school, it appeared difficult and expensive for my father to afford the high school fees required for one to be a boarder. There was, however, a provision for one to be a day student which was relatively cheaper. I opted to be a day student which meant I had to walk 44 kilometers to and from school. I had to leave home fairly early around 4 a.m. in order to be in school on time. It was a very exhausting exercise because more often than not I did without a meal at lunch time. After the first term of school, my father decided that I put up with one of his relatives that lived a few kilometers from the school. This was a big relief for me to concentrate more on my studies.

The intermediate school level was quite challenging. During the four years our curriculum was organized to prepare us for the Kenya African Preliminary Examination, a national examination which was used to select students for entry into secondary schools. The number of secondary schools in the then Kenya colony were twelve in number. The competition for the few places in these secondary schools, as can be imagined was extremely stiff. Teaching facilities and materials were not a problem as they were provided by the government. Most teachers were fairly well qualified, although teaching through rote memory was still the order of the day. Discipline was rigidly maintained through caning or working in the school farm during class hours.

An interesting element of the intermediate school, was that it was not purely academic. It also had a prevocational element in which students were expected to learn agriculture and carpentry for boys and home science for girls. The colonial government's educational perception for these subjects was that they were useful in combating attitudes of intellectual arrogance of students, which come with purely an academic nature curriculum, and that the subjects would help school leavers to become self employed when they complete school. In this regard, my intermediate school had a school farm with coffee and bananas plantations, a team of oxen for ploughing and a fully equipped carpentry workshop. As students, we however, hardly appreciated these subjects. They actually meant a lot of manual work which at times interfered with class work. Second, farm work was often used as a form of punishment. Related to this, since the school had not employed a herdsman to herd the oxen, students were routinely selected to herd, which meant missing a day's classes altogether. Third, these subjects were not examinable. An important incident which brought a lot of joy to the students and virtually terminated practical agriculture in the school was, when the oxen were stolen one night and the school failed to recover them. The students were exceedingly happy about it.

After completing the intermediate school, I passed the Kenya African Preliminary Examination to join a new secondary school, 36 kilometers from my home where we were pioneers. This was in 1962, a year before Kenya attained its independence. By then my father was very sickly and the problem of school fees became even more critical. My mother through her petty trade of brewing some local beer, managed to raise my first term's school fees, but the situation became even worse as my father passed away after hardly a month's stay at my new school. I contemplated abandoning secondary school and seek a place at a primary teachers college, where no fee was required. My mother advised me against such a decision and instead encouraged me to continue with secondary education, promising to redouble her efforts in brewing beer and seeking financial assistance which was normally given to orphaned children who were in secondary schools by the county council. A few relatives came to her assistance to pay my fees for the remaining school terms and begin form two of the secondary school. Fortunately, her application to the County Council of Bungoma for financial assistance was also successful. Although the assistance was partial, it greatly supplemented the meagre income from brewing beer.

Kibabii Secondary School which I had joined, was among the few new secondary schools opened in Bungoma District. Although it had most teaching facilities particularly tuition blocks, which originally belonged to a primary teachers college, it lacked one basic facility, namely, a science laboratory, this made it difficult for the school to offer physics, chemistry and biology as separate subjects. As a pioneer class, we were therefore offered general science among other subjects in preparation for the Cambridge Overseas School Certificate Examination set by the University of Cambridge Examination Syndicate in Britain. This examination which was then taken in form four was critical in determining whether one would continue to the advanced level or high school in preparation for university or to terminate ones studies and seek some training or employment. As a pioneer class, preparation for this examination gave us considerable anxiety not only because some of the facilities were lacking, but also the quality of our teaching staff. The school was staffed mainly by dedicated Dutch Marian Brothers and a couple of non-graduate African teachers. In our mistaken perception, our teaching staff was of poor quality. First, because the Brothers were Dutch and they had little or no experience with the British system of education in general and the Cambridge Examination in particular. Second, the non-graduate African teachers were unfit to teach at the secondary school level because they had trained as primary school teachers. With this kind of teaching staff, we felt the whole class was doomed to fail. In Form 2 in 1963, we decided to strike against our teachers. The strike lasted for three weeks, but back home I was very much ostracised by friends and relatives for foolishly joining a senseless strike without appreciating the poor state of our home and the efforts that were being made to give me good education. Fortunately I was not expelled from the school.

The strike had no effect on changing the quality of our teachers. They were a very committed team and did their best to familiarize themselves with the Cambridge Overseas Examinations syllabus. To everyones delight, when our class took this examination in 1965, most of the students scored very high grades and Kibabii Secondary School was first in Bungoma District and among the best in Nyanza Province. I obtained a Division One in this examination. The big lesson I learnt from the Dutch Brothers and the African teachers was commitment and dedication to one's work. They were very excellent and I really emulated their work especially the headmaster who taught us mathematics and Christian religious education. Among my best sport was soccer in which I served as a goalkeeper.

On the strength of my performance at 'O' level examination (Cambridge Overseas School Certificate), I was selected to join Form 5 at Nyeri High school in Central Province in 1966. It was a very exciting experience since I had not done my studies outside our province and district. Fortunately this time round, the issue of tuition fees was not a problem. The independent government in a bid to meet the demands for highly skilled manpower, had decreed that education at Forms 5 and 6 which were university preparatory classes, had to be free. Students in these classes were only expected to pay the 'A' level examination fee, but the government through the high schools provided all the learning materials.

Life in high school was less exciting than at secondary level. There was less dependence on teachers who seemed mainly to guide us on what to study. The academic work was quite demanding. I opted to study geography, history, mathematics and Bible studies, the latter which I studied privately because it was not formally offered by Nyeri High School. I passed the Cambridge Overseas Advanced Examination which I took in 1967 and qualified for entry into the University of East Africa which comprised of colleges at Makerere in Uganda, Nairobi in Kenya and Dar-es-Salaam in Tanzania.

As it is the practice, students make selections for university studies during their last year of high school. In my time, employment opportunities were many because Kenya had just emerged from colonialism in 1963, and hence there was a high demand for skilled manpower in the various sectors of the economy and the government. Many careers were therefore open to me unlike the situation today where openings for employment have become extremely limited.

With a wide range of career openings, selection for my occupation appeared difficult. After a careful consideration, however, I selected teaching. It meant I had to pursue a Bachelor of Education (B.Ed.) degree which was only available at Makerere. This was a professional three year degree which had been started in response to the shortage of secondary school teachers in East Africa. It was considered to be a cheaper way of producing secondary school teachers than the traditional British system which required an extra year of a postgraduate diploma after completing a B.A. or B.Sc.

There were a number of reasons that influenced my decision to become a teacher. First, in the colonial period in Kenya as elsewhere in Africa, teaching was among the few occupations open to most Africans. Therefore throughout my schooling I had interacted with many teachers, both good and bad ones. The good teachers were a strong source of inspiration to me. They imparted knowledge superbly well and were highly respected in schools as well as the wider community. Second, I selected the teaching profession because I felt it could provide me with the opportunity to work near my rural home since there were several secondary schools in my province.

In June 1968, I joined Makerere University College for a B.Ed. degree course. I opted to study geography and history as academic subjects. Professional courses in education included: pedagogy, history of education, sociology of education, educational psychology, philosophy of education and comparative education all which were compulsory. There was an optional course, "Primary Schools Methods" which was given to a small number of students interested in teaching in primary teachers' colleges. I opted for it. During the three year study we also had to take two six week sessions of teaching practice in secondary schools or primary teachers colleges.

Life at Makerere was quite challenging, but equally enriching. As students we participated in many academic and non-academic activities. I particularly enjoyed campus politics and public lecturers occasionally delivered by leading personalities from many parts of the world. The lively Makerere atmosphere inspired me to feel that I should subsequently become a university lecturer if I performed well in my final university examination. Because the number of graduate studies was relatively small and the East African governments were keen to train highly skilled manpower, the Kenya government offered us very generous scholarships which often assisted me to pay school fees for some of my brothers.

At Makerere, like in other constituent colleges of the University of East Africa, degrees were classified into four; namely, first class honours, second class honours upper and lower divisions, and pass. In the final university examination in February/March, 1971, I scored a second class honours, upper-division which qualified me to pursue a Master's degree.

On leaving Makerere in March, 1971, I was posted to Kaimosi Primary Teachers' College in Western Province. The college, like twenty others in the country, offers a two year programme for teachers preparing to teach in the primary schools. Teaching at this college was equally challenging, but interesting. Although I had not taught at the primary school level, I had to cope with the demands of not only teaching students how to teach, but had the additional responsibility of supervising their teaching practice in primary schools. This gave me a real experience with many of our primary schools which have poor teaching facilities and materials.

In November 1971 I was offered a scholarship to pursue a Master of Arts (Education) degree by the University of Nairobi. The Faculty of Education which was relatively new was pioneering in postgraduate studies for its staff development. It had no organized coursework programmes, therefore students were expected to do their master's degree by thesis only. This proved quite difficult because I had to learn the canons of educational research through self-teaching. For my thesis I researched on the impact of the new primary approach on the quality of teaching in primary schools in Kenya. This was a programme which had been introduced in schools to promote pupil centered learning. Thesis writing was a very frustrating experience. This was particularly the case at the proposal writing stage when I received very harsh comments on my proposal at a staff seminar I felt like having reached the end of the world. But some of the teachers gave me a lot of encouragement privately. On completion of the thesis I was offered an appointment as a tutorial fellow or teaching assistant in the Faculty of Education, University of Nairobi in November 1973.

Since my time, master's programmes in the national universities have considerably improved. Although small numbers of students are still admitted into the programmes for staff development, they now do their studies by course work and thesis writing. There have, however, been several crash programmes in which students did their master's by coursework only to prepare them as tutors for primary and secondary teachers' colleges. The rationale behind these programmes was that master's degree studies which require coursework and thesis writing are specifically meant for university staff development and because of some logistical problems, students take more than two years to complete their studies. Although on the overall, the quality of students has been on the decline the quality of supervision by some lecturers is equally poor. The morale is low due to poor working conditions. Consequently, it takes some of them as long as five months to give feedback to students work. Despite these problems, I have not joined this category of teachers for I do give my feedback to student's work very promptly and this can be attested by the number of postgraduate students I have supervised both at Master's and doctoral levels.

Although my tutorial fellowship required me to conduct tutorials only, due to staff shortages in the faculty, I had to give lectures as well. At the same time I registered for the Doctor of Philosophy degree which again was by thesis only in February 1974. My experience with the master's degree proved extremely useful. I investigated into factors that determine teaching effectiveness in primary schools.

I worked as a tutorial fellow for about one and half years and I was promoted to the position of lecturer in 1975. The basic requirement for this post was a doctorate degree, but due to problems of staffing, this requirement was waived and has continued to be so because of the recent rapid expansion of university education in the country. In my promotion, I however, had an advantage because I had reorganized my master's thesis for publication into a book. The harsh criticisms I received when I presented my master's proposal was my first baptism of fire. Thanks also to my former lecturers and friend at Makerere who encouraged me never to fear harsh comments in seminars. I learnt to take comments on my papers positively and used them to improve several of my papers for publication. My lecturer friend always insisted 'that until you have put your thoughts on paper nobody would have grounds to talk about them'. At the same time I joined the Historical Association of Kenya which held staff seminars more regularly, and there comments and criticisms on papers were even more savage than I thought. This made me a battle hardened young academician.

In July 1979, I was promoted to the post of Senior Lecturer in the Department of Educational Foundations at Kenyatta University. The basic requirements for this post are: a doctorate degree, evidence of continued research and publications in the form of a book or articles in refereed journals. What was spectacular about this appointment was that I was appointed in absentia without attending the interview over three colleagues contending for the job because of these publications, and there was some intrigue to deny me the job. I had no difficulty in getting appointed to this post because I had by then published two books and I also had several articles in refereed journals. Similar conditions apply to the post of associate professor although in this particular case more publications are required. I was appointed to this post in February 1984.

At the professorial level, the basic requirements are: a doctorate degree, five years of teaching since appointment as associate professor or twelve years of university teaching in the post of lecturer or above, evidence of continuous research and publications which include at least two books or six articles in refereed journals since appointment to associate professor post, and academic leadership and administrative experience. In August 1988, I had fulfilled all these conditions and I was appointed to post of professor. The process of appointment also includes an external assessment of the applicants publications and academic record. In all honesty, this was the most difficult interview I ever attended, because the first oral question posed by the chairman was very devastating. The question sounded simple but well calculated. It was stated that from my curriculum vitae, I had carried out many researches and published my works. In this process, which is the most difficult problem I have ever faced during my research exercises? I felt that this question was meant to derail me because among the panel members, I was becoming a professor at a very young age (44 years). Once again my persistent efforts in publishing and research helped to sail through. I also wish to point out that my scholarship has earned me appointments at professorial levels at Universities of Swaziland, and Papua New Guinea.

I should, however, point out that following the mushrooming of universities in Kenya since the late 1980s these promotion conditions, especially those that pertain to publications have been grossly violated because of competition between the national universities in the appointments of senior positions and political considerations. Consequently we now have many senior lecturers and professors who have not done research and published and yet they have not "perished!"

Responsibilities for senior positions are basically the same. My duties in the Department of Educational Foundations at Kenyatta University include: teaching B.Ed. students, courses in comparative education, history of education and sociology of education. These undergraduate students take other educational courses in the Departments of Psychology, Administration, Planning and Curriculum Development and Communications and Technology and teaching subjects in the Faculties of Arts, Science, Environmental Studies and Commerce.

They are being prepared as secondary school teachers, although a small number is being prepared to teach in primary teachers colleges. The B.Ed. degree is also offered at other national universities, namely Egerton, Moi, Nairobi, and Maseno University College. My responsibilities also include teaching postgraduate students namely M.A. (Education) and M.Ed. degrees as well as supervising their theses and those of doctoral candidates. There are administrative and academic duties pertaining to the Senate of the University. From 1986 to 1990 I was chairman of the department and I initiated a very successful Postgraduate Studies Committee in which all postgraduate students in the faculty present their proposals. I am fairly popular with my students because I always do my best to obtain current data on issues and present my lectures with a sense of humour.

Academic staff are expected by the university to conduct research and publish, attend seminars and conferences as well as participation in professional organizations and other bodies dealing with the development of the country. I should, however, point out that due to heavy teaching loads and scarcity of funds, many colleagues are not involved in these activities. Personally, I have not been faced with this particular problem very seriously, largely because my expertise and experience have earned me a good number of external research grants and some consultancies with NGOs and several donor organizations.

I have personally been engaged in a number of professional organizations; for example, the Kenya Institute of Education Governing Council of which I was chairman, and I have coordinated several national and regional research projects. I have also received awards and fellowships for short term studies in the U.S.A., the United Kingdom and Germany, and I have traveled to conferences in the Netherlands, Canada, France, Italy, Brunei, and to a number of the African countries. I have also been an external examiner to many of the regional universities. Through some of my contacts, Kenyatta University, has acquired fellowships and some vital teaching equipment.

I am married with five children: three daughters and two sons.

Becoming A Teacher Educator In Kuwait

Salwa Al-Jassar
Kuwait

My name is Salwa Al Jassar, I was born in 1959. My nationality is Kuwaiti. I graduated from Kuwait University in 1980 and received my Ph.D. from University of Pittsburgh in 1991. I am now a member of the Faculty of Education, Kuwait University and the Director of the Curricula Textbooks Department, Ministry of Education, Kuwait.

Before talking about my long journey in the field of education and how I became a teacher educator, I'd like you to be acquainted with my country, Kuwait. Kuwait lies in Asia, on the north west of the Arabian Gulf. A small country with a population of one and a half million, but great in its educational achievements (illiteracy ratio is no more than 2%). Since the 1930's, Kuwait has witnessed a remarkable development in the fields of education.

The beginnings of education in Kuwait

In 1887, informal education started in my country. In 1912 the first organized school was founded. In 1936, the Council of Education was founded. Education was organized and plans for syllabuses were laid down. From 1956 to 1972 there was an increase in numbers of schools, the first five year plan of education issued, the education ladder had been established to include kindergarten, primary, intermediate, and secondary levels, followed by the university.

Education in Kuwait aims at achieving integration between the plans of education and the requirements of the State comprehensive plan to achieve the following: a) manpower needed for economic and social development, b) realizing national needs in both cultural and scientific areas, c) achieving interaction between cultural and science development and up-to-date methodologies, d) consolidating cultural relations with other countries, e) keeping pace with modern approaches of education and science technology, and f) preparing good teachers.

The educational ladder in Kuwait is divided into four stages: kindergarten starting at the age of four, primary starting at the age of six for four years, intermediate starting at the age of ten for four years, and secondary starting at the age of fourteen for four years. The primary, intermediate and secondary stages are compulsory.

The professional experiences I had that led me to my current position

After my graduation from Kuwait University, I worked as a social studies teacher for five years; two in an intermediate school and the other three in a unit/credit secondary school. It took me a year and a half to get my special diploma in education.

To be a teacher educator, the educational system in Kuwait University required me to study, on a scholarship, for at least five years which lead to M.A. and Ph.D. degrees specialized in teacher education programme or curriculum and instruction specified in subject matter. So I was deeply indulged with interest to exert my effort to get my M.A. which I obtained from Michigan State University in 1987. Afterwards, I continued to fulfill my requirements for the Ph.D. degree which I received from the University of Pittsburgh in the teacher education programme.

Since then, I started my career at the Faculty of Education, Kuwait University. Now, I am teaching students who will be teachers (teacher-students) in social studies teaching methods, curricula, and student teaching seminars. I also supervise students during their training trips in the public schools for at least six to eight visits during the training sessions. In addition to my work as a teacher educator, I am an academic supervisor at the Curricula Department, Ministry of Education since 1991.

In addition to the above mentioned career I have done research and prepared a syllabus course description for the curriculum and methodology department, developed teacher training programmes in the faculty, wrote a study entitled," Who the Effective Teacher Is," evaluated attainment techniques of the primary school pupils, developed a criterion to measure the efficiency of the teachers of computers, and revised the social studies curricula in the intermediate stage from the disciplinary prospective to the national one.

The academic and nonacademic activities

I am a member of the National Council of Social Studies, Kuwaiti Teacher Society, Consultant Councils in The Faculty of Education, ELT Committee for the Primary Stage, Development and Evaluation Committees, a training programme for qualifying senior teachers, school principals and vice principals, seminars with the Faculty Staffs, Parents Board in the Universal American School, Kuwait University Staffs Society, and Supreme Committee for organizing the curricula and methodology conference and rapporteur of the media committee

I was a co-writer of social studies textbooks for the fourth year primary, wrote a course description M.A. programme in the Faculty of Education, reported the Ministry of Education achievements for the academic year 1994 to be submitted to the UNESCO, programmed local and international conferences, participated in field trips to government schools, and headed the technical committee of Uhod Model Kindergarten, and evaluating Faculty of Education Programmes.

The objectives of the courses I teach in the Curriculum and Instruction Department, Faculty of Education, Kuwait University

In the social studies teaching methods course student teacher should be able to accomplish the following objects: to become more aware of the three major sources of objectives of the school curriculum, to be able to understand the three domains, when provided with a list of examples of the objectives of these domains (cognitive, affective, and psychomotor) be able to write a lesson plan, be able to understand the planning and implementing variety of teaching techniques, be able to understand classroom organizational patterns through identifying the pattern as competitive, cooperative or individual, be able to understand measurement and evaluation to command knowledge in the subject matter that be taught.

In the curriculum courses the preservice teacher should be able to understand the following: theoretical knowledge about learning and human behavior, curriculum design and implementation, a variety of curriculum integration ranging from concurrent teaching of related subjects, learning skills helpful in acquiring the

105

curriculum content being taught, and strategies of developing and evaluating school curriculum

Upon completion of the students teaching (seminar) courses a preservice teacher should be able to accomplish the following objectives: understand factors involved in classroom incidents that related to teacher characteristics, classroom organization, and classroom environment, select appropriate information gathering instruments when seeking to make any research in social studies teaching, practice and analyse existing classroom learning activities, discuss different issues in social studies teaching methods, and have a command of theoretical knowledge about research methods.

In short, to become a teacher educator at Kuwait University a person must meet the requirements of a university degree in a certain major, a M.A. in curricula and methodology and finally a Ph.D. from an accredited university. These are the minimum requirements for individuals to be teacher educators in addition to supervising teaching practice.

A New Zealander

Bob O'Brien
New Zealand

When I made my first contact with the New Zealand state education system during World War II important changes were being made to the 1877 Education Act. Free, compulsory and secular education became the requirement for all children under the age of fifteen. My generation (b. 1934) would be the first to benefit from a provision for automatic access to secondary schooling. It would also be the depression-depleted generation that would have to supply the teaching force needed to deliver the revised curriculum to the rapidly expanding population of these two small South Pacific Islands over the next two decades. The doors of opportunity opened easily for me and my contemporaries, so my career in teaching and teacher education reflects the particular circumstances of this time rather than that of a typical New Zealand model.

By the mid 1990s I held the position of Director, School of Secondary Education at Wellington College of Education, Te Whanau o Ako Pai ki te Upoko o te Ika, the only teacher education facility available in the capital city of New Zealand (pop. 325,000). My role was to manage the pre-service training of about forty to fifty graduates through a one year programme. I became a teacher educator in 1980 after living and working in the suburbs of the city for most of my career. Because my early life and schooling was also experienced in suburban Wellington I had no contact of significance with the indigenous people of my homeland, the Maori, until I entered Wellington Teachers College in 1952.

The Maori had their own extended family model (*hapu*) of educating their young in the customs and values of their tribe (*iwi*), but after a century of invasion and domination by, in the main, Anglo-Saxon settlers, they remained in rural areas. Native schools had been opened to hasten the assimilation of Maori into *Pakeha* (European) life but as they were inevitably sited in remote districts they did not succeed in spite of much effort on the part of many teachers who served in them. By the 1950s the issues were not bi-culturalism, multi-culturalism nor equity, but rather the recruitment of teachers, the funding to build the many schools now needed and the conditions of service required to attract and retain competent, able people in the teaching force. The Maori were no better served in these times than they had been at any other period since *Pakeha* colonisation began in 1840.

I was the first of my family to experience five years of secondary schooling. Even though one of my grandmothers had been a teacher, my own parents, uncles and aunts had limited educational opportunities. The 1944 Act had made provision for universal education up to fifteen years of age but had also created a system of public examinations which I had to negotiate in my last three years at Rongotai College. School Certificate, designed to achieve never more than a fifty percent pass rate among candidates, was the minimal entry requirement for teacher training at that time, so I, as a male and a holder of a Higher School Certificate was a member of an under-represented group among those whom I joined for a two year primary teacher training course at Wellington Teachers College (1952-53). I also enrolled at Victoria University as a part-time student to discover if a degree and a later transfer to secondary school teaching was a possibility. I would only acquire a Trained Teacher's Certificate after my training and one year as a probationary teacher, but that would be sufficient to launch me on a secure career as a primary school teacher. I soon discovered that a degree by itself was a sufficient entry qualification for access to secondary school teaching for it was not until 1987 that specific training for the work became obligatory.

However, such was the growing shortage of secondary school teachers that even before I had completed my first degree, my old school, Rongotai College, had invited me to transfer to the senior school after three years of teaching 11-13 year old boys the general primary curriculum. At the end of that year (1958) I completed my bachelor's degree through continued part-time study and taught English, geography and social studies to a range of classes at different levels. Many of my colleagues at Rongotai had followed a similar path into secondary school teaching and several had begun but never completed a second degree. It was not until the 1980s that supply/demand factors began to force potential teachers to become more qualification conscious.

After traveling in Europe and teaching intermittently in north London schools during 1960 I returned to Rongotai and more part-time study. With a completed master's degree in English and acknowledged competence as a teacher I was well placed to advance my career provided that I was willing to move to other places. The New Zealand service at that time (1962) had salary bars in place as a means of fostering the popularity of teaching in rural areas, so the recently married O'Briens decided that the Cook Islands would be a challenging but interesting option that met the 'Country Service' requirement. These islands are near neighbours to New Zealand and had been annexed by the new Dominion in 1901. The colonial power delayed the provision of secondary education for the majority of the children of the islands for over half a century but by the time that I arrived at Rarotonga in 1964, Tereora College was thriving and popular. I enjoyed teaching and acting in a middle management role at the school. As an English teacher I was confronted with the problem that for nearly all students, and some of my colleagues, the first language was Cook Island Maori. Furthermore, far-reaching political and economic changes were also taking place at this time and so the curriculum and the very structure of the education system were frequent topics of reflection and debate.

After a two year tour of duty in the Cook Islands I returned to my homeland and accepted a position as Head of the English Department of Wainuiomata College, about 30 kilometres from downtown Wellington. In this, I followed another fairly common pattern of New Zealand teacher behaviour. Some went to the country, liked the lifestyle, and stayed. Others looked for promotion and other professional options by making an astute and timely return to metropolitan New Zealand. But with a steady decline in rural population, and a rapidly growing shortage of teachers in urban schools, the 'Country Service' regulations were abandoned so I was among the last to have my professional development shaped in this way. Most of the people involved in teacher education up to that point would have had met the rural service condition earlier in their careers and so it should be acknowledged as an important factor in the general preparation of teachers for several generations. Being prepared to teach in a sole charge or two teacher school was a noteworthy characteristic of the training process for New Zealanders and perhaps helps explain why most classrooms are still managed as they are. By 1964 the national population had stabilised at around three million but was unevenly distributed over the two main islands, with most found in the vicinity of Auckland, the northernmost city. Wainuiomata was a typical community of this era. A small, long-established settlement had become the core of a rapidly developing residential area which in this case housed immigrants from Maori communities from the east coast of North Island, ex-patriate English, Scots, Irish, Dutch, Samoan and other Pacific Islanders.

New primary and secondary schools were having to be built at pace and often the construction workers shared the site with the teachers for many years after the first pupils had arrived. This was certainly the case with me at Wainuiomata for most of my fourteen years there. During that phase of my career I saw Wainuiomata College student roll numbers peak at around 1100 in the mid-seventies and then begin a decline to half of that number by the late eighties. Teachers learned to cope with over-crowded, under-resourced classrooms, occasional syllabus amendments and an increasingly multi-cultural population before retrenchment brought a new set of challenges. Many teachers expressed their concerns about the future of education in New Zealand through their national association. I was one of them. Through this activity I came to membership of the Teachers Refresher Course Committee and a formal point of contact with the whole field of teacher education. Both pre-service and in-service business became one of my major professional interests and provided me with the preparation that I felt that I needed to justify my transfer to the Hutt Valley Centre for the training of secondary school teachers in 1980. This outpost of Christchurch Teachers College had been set up in 1969 to help relieve the extreme staffing difficulties that beset many parts of New Zealand at that time. Auckland and Christchurch had been the only secondary teacher training sites until then and new arrangements were politically essential. Many models of training were examined and some were tried. Recruiting from abroad was tried. The Outpost, as it became known, provided training for 10-40 people unable to spend a year of post-graduate training at either of the two traditional colleges. I had been a member of the Working Party which developed a school-based training programme which demonstrated that an effective partnership between pre-service teacher educators and experienced

110

practising teachers could be forged and that effectively trained beginning teachers could be supplied for duty in the schools of the Greater Wellington area. The other relevant experiences that I had accumulated while teaching at Wainuiomata which probably assisted in this appointment as a teacher educator included: involvement in a major reform of the English syllabus; the promotion of drama as a vehicle for effective learning; contributions to the growing debate about and development of assessment and reporting procedures; the adaptation and promotion of a workshop programme intended to help adults (teachers) and adolescents improve their inter-personal communication skills; and support for the drive to have New Zealand schools acknowledge their obligations to the maintenance of Maori language and culture. My Refresher Course Committee work had extended my awareness of the other sectors within New Zealand education and required me to advance my understanding about adult learners. Participation on a Working Party that had reported on the state of New Zealand education in respect of a UNESCO enquiry into education for international understanding had reminded me of my country's size, affluence and isolation.

The teacher training programme that I accepted responsibility to manage and teach in had evolved through the seventies but was still firmly within the parameters identified by the original Working Party. As well as the traditional university graduates the programme was developed to train teachers of technical and commercial subjects drawn from a section of the community which had, almost without exception, received its earlier tertiary education at polytechnics. Thus the breadth of experiences and the diversity of backgrounds of the trainees, together with their generally strong commitment to want to learn to teach effectively, meant that the annual intake was, of itself, a major contributor to the training that went on. At the end of the courses in December of each year successful trainees were awarded a Diploma of Teaching (Secondary) which enabled them to seek employment as Provisionally Registered Teachers. Only a small number of trainees withdrew from the Outpost programme and a high proportion went on to teach and remain teachers for an appreciable period.

Reviews of the programme were made in 1975, 1981 and 1990 by differing agencies and all found that the partnership between Outpost and schools had worked to the mutual advantage of all except a small number of trainees and teachers. The maintenance of this relationship was seen to be the main task of the Director apart from the daily organisation and long-term planning. After 1987 the programme was co-ordinated and partly delivered from the Wellington College of Education, a campus less centrally sited in Greater Wellington than the Outpost, and so the distribution of schools involved changed, too.

The physical transfer meant that for the first time in the Wellington area all teacher education (pre- and in-service) would be co-ordinated by the one institution. Wellington College of Education had become autonomous after a major reorganisation of the administration of education in New Zealand that began in 1989 and still continues. Higher standards of academic achievement have been introduced and traditional time-frames for the pre-service training of teachers have been amended. A Bachelor of Education Degree has been developed conjointly with Victoria University of Wellington. The School of Secondary Education, along with the other Schools within the College, is currently devising responses to the newly promulgated Curriculum Framework (1993). Substantial, overt changes are occurring in all sectors of New Zealand education and the challenge for teacher educators is to monitor them and reflect upon the implications of these developments for the next generation of teachers. The small team of faculty members who contribute to the programme traditionally work in a part-time capacity with the director. The School of Secondary Education does not have a high profile within the college in either academic or extra-curricular fields. The Director performs most of the administrative roles and does a little teaching but shares the supervision of trainee practica with his colleagues who were all experienced, highly regarded secondary school teachers who happened to be available on the intermittent occasions that their services could be advantageous. They interacted with the trainees at WCE and in schools, where they also attempted to re-inforce the concept of the partnership between the two agencies. The part-time faculty have also been involved in many of the curriculum and qualification developments that have been organised nationally since 1993. Their leadership and expertise has been recognised and has strengthened the reputation of the School at a time when New Zealand education, as in many parts of the world, is in a state of flux. It seems that the egalitarian precepts which underpinned developments in New Zealand education after World War Two are no longer politically powerful. At a time when school populations are going to increase there is a mismatch between the avowed importance of education to the nation's future and the resources supplied by the state. The attitude of a significant proportion of parents and their children towards schools and teachers diminishes the status of education in the community and does little to encourage the more able members of the adolescent age group to contemplate a career in teaching.

Today's students are only too aware of the consequences for teachers and school administrators of the stresses arising from substantial reforms in educational administration, curriculum revision and a radically restructured national qualifications framework. It is not going to be easy to attract enough recruits for teacher education in the coming years. Without a teaching force of improving quality and a steady infusion of keen, able new-comers to the profession then there must be great uncertainty about the achievement of the outcomes predicted by the advocates of the reforms of the past decade. Such pessimism is reinforced by the moves towards 'user pays' in the tertiary education. It is unlikely that would-be teachers will be given incentives to be trained and unless the status and conditions of service of teachers are improved it is conceivable that with the continued pre-eminence of 'market forces' in the economy the collapse of the generally egalitarian state school system and the shift of responsibility for education to the private sector will be the next major development. In such a scenario the place of teacher education could well be diminished and the stimuli arising from the decade of reforms will be dulled.

Teacher Education In Papua New Guinea

Michael Kautia Popo
Papua New Guinea

This is a personal story of how I became a teacher educator and the nature of my work. I was born in 1948 and have been in education since 1968.

I am working in the Community Teachers College. There are eight community teachers colleges in Papua New Guinea. We train teachers to teach in the community (primary) schools. The students entering teachers college are grade 10 school leavers ranging in ages from seventeen to twenty years. The college also accepts non school leavers. After three years of training the students graduate with Diploma in teaching as generalist teachers. Hence they are taught content knowledge and methods in teaching English, mathematics, science, community life, professional studies, expressive arts, physical education, health and religion studies. Each subject is taught by different people who specialise in that subject. My specialist subject is mathematics. Thus I teach mathematics to year one and two students. Opportunities are provided for the students to practice skills in teaching in the practicum sessions. When they graduate we expect them to be responsible and reflective teachers.

While at the college the students are encouraged to organize social activities for themselves and take part in the outside sports, so that their college life is enjoyable, relaxing and meaningful.

As an educational institution the college expects me to attend and participate actively in any staff development workshops organized by the National Department of Education (NDOE) and to contribute positively to in-college inservice and strand meetings. The institution expects in principle for me to attend educational conferences and seminars in-country or off-shore; however, lack of funds makes it difficult for this expectation to be realized. I am also required to involve actively in the community school inservice as resources person.

I work in the residential college, hence the institution as well as the government expects me to supervise community service three afternoons a week. This is in line with the government policy in developing attitudes of self reliance and responsibility in the students. Lack of funding to hire more ancillary staff to take care of colleges grounds, maintenance work, students mess is one of the reason why we do community service. I am also required to be on duty once a fortnight.

My involvement in education began in 1966 when I enrolled at Port Moresby Teachers College to be trained as community school teacher. I graduated with a teachers certificate the following year and commenced teaching in 1968. After four and half years out in the field I was selected for six months inservice course at St. Paul's Teachers College. At the completion of the course I was awarded Diploma in school management and organization. Before becoming a teacher educator I worked as class teacher, senior teacher and headmaster in community schools.

The need for localization in teachers colleges in PNG was recognised in early 1970s. Hence the NDOE in consultation with the University of Papua New Guinea (UPNG) designed a inservice packet known as Diploma in Education Studies (DES) Tertiary to prepare nationals for lecturing jobs. This was a two year course jointly run by the University of Papua New Guinea and the Staff Development Unit of the NDOE.

The course is advertised in a special education gazette in March each year. Experienced community school teachers then apply for the course. The criteria for the selection are: candidate must be a senior teacher or headmaster, five years of teaching experience, superior teaching report, and at least grade 10 qualification.

The selected candidates would do one year internship in the Teachers College in PNG as associate lecturers. The second year would be spend in Canberra College of Advanced Education-Australia. On completion of the course candidates are awarded Diploma in Education Studies (Tertiary) Teaching by UPNG. This is the process I went through to become a teacher educator in 1979-1981.

There have been changes made to DES (Tertiary) course. The DES course was replaced by B.Ed. (Tertiary) course in 1987. The B.Ed. (Tertiary) course is a

116

three year course. The graduates receive the B.Ed. (Tertiary) degree upon successfully completing the course. It is the Education Department requirement that teacher educators must have first degree. Hence the Ddiploma holders like myself are encouraged to undertake B.Ed. (Inservice) course to qualify for degree B.Ed. (Inservice) course is of two year duration.

This changing requirement in necessary because the teachers college course has changed from a two year certificate course to a three year diploma course. It is anticipated that in the near future colleges would be selecting students from National High School who have completed grade 12. Thus this is a challenge and treat to the teacher educators in Community Teachers College.

Teacher Educators in PNG work very hard in academic and non academic activities but pay is poor. Lack of resource materials hinders lecturers to function effectively. These coupled with many other problems have forced significant number of teacher educators seek employment in international education agencies and in private sectors.

Unless measures are taken to control this trend teachers colleges stand to lose more lecturers to international education agencies and private sector.

My Pedagogical Autobiography

Elena Pavlova
Russia

I, Elena Pavlova, instructor of the Sub-department of Teacher's Oral Skills (word by word: Teacher's Culture of Speech) at the Moscow State Pedagogical University, with all responsibility state that I became a teacher, and what is more, a teacher educator, absolutely by chance. At least, I was quite sure about that up to the very moment when the authors of this book asked me to describe how I had become a teacher in a teacher training school and how it normally happens in our country.

Humanities have always come to my heart's content. That's why, when I was to choose an institution of higher learning, I turned to a list of higher schools which curricula included literature, languages, and history. In Moscow, you could count them on the fingers of one hand; these were the Moscow State University, the Institute of Foreign Languages, the Institute of Foreign Relations, the History and Archives' Institute, and two teacher training institutions of higher learning.

The Moscow University's philological department was, at that time, the most prestigious and hence, projectionist one; for example, a pull-in or a bribe normally weighed more than actual aptitude or an educational level of an applicant. Nevertheless, I decided to take a risk knowing that if I failed I would try something else (entry exams to the Moscow University were held a month earlier than to most higher schools).

And I did fail, missing 1.5 scores out of the required pass mark. This was the only reason for my applying to the Russian Language and Literature Department of the Moscow State Pedagogical Institute (currently the Moscow State Pedagogical University) whose curriculum largely coincided with one of the University and the entry exams were quite the same (composition, Russian Language (oral), literature (oral), history, and foreign language).

Although there were approximately 7.6 contenders for one seat, I managed to get a passing mark and, at the age of 16, became a student of a teacher training institute, to teach children or whoever else. It should be mentioned here that most of the girls, who were in the same year as I, also viewed training there as a good chance to get a higher school diploma in humanities, and cherished no illusions about their future profession.

These were years of interesting and easy learning. All subjects which made up the curriculum were obligatory and rather evenly distributed among 10 semesters comprising the required five years of higher schooling. If mastered, the curriculum provided for students' knowledge that actually was not so bad. A future teacher of Russian Language and Literature was supposed to learn the Church Slavonic and the Old Russian Languages, Latin, historical grammar, Modern Russian Language, Russian literature (from ancient times to 1917), Soviet literature, World literature (from the antiquity to the modern times), general linguistics, literary criticism, and psychology.

The curriculum also included a set of career-oriented courses, such as methods of teaching the Russian Language and Literature, age physiology, history of educational science, theory and practice of communist up-bringing, as well as inevitable ideological subjects. The latter circle consisted of history of the Communist Party of the Soviet Union, historical and dialectical materialism atheism, scientific communism, and political economy of capitalism and socialism. However, these subjects raised an ironical smile in the vast majority of students who laughed up their sleeves saying, "How can you turn a pedagogical institute into a normal institution of higher learning? Only by eliminating all courses related to education." (Marxism then was a sort of taboo; it was considered an obligatory subject even in ballet schools.)

The first three years of learning were aimed at developing students' philological and general cultural competence. My interests were in linguistics;

120

although the Church Slavonic Language was most close to my heart, I was strongly taken by the world literature. Teaching methods, both in theory and in practice, were introduced after the third year of training. Practical training normally began with one or two months of working in a pioneer camp as a "Young Pioneer leader" (this was called the "Practice of Communist Up-Bringing", students worked for free). For another month, students attended classes held by proficient teachers in basic schools, and after that they were to conduct a class of literature and one of the Russian Language by themselves.

Unfortunately, space limitations of this article prevent me from giving more detail about that (hence, American readers will not find here a chronicle of events in a madhouse based in the Thriller-Land which would otherwise be presented).

In short, all this practice produced such an impression on me that I eventually decided to try all my efforts to escape from being employed by a school.

The only one real chance was to pass on from the day department to the evening one a year before leaving the institute. Students who attended evening classes were not subject to an obligatory three-year employment in accordance with the specialisation received. After an evening course, one could also take up a related profession; for example, work as a librarian, laboratory assistant in a research institution or fill a position in a department of the same higher school you had graduated from. The latter option was most attractive. This meant that after several years of idiotic work with documents, an individual would finally receive a reward; namely, a recommendation which made it possible to take a day-time post-graduate course. And this, in its turn, paved the way to joining the department's faculty as its active member.

However, protection mattered much even in this case. To receive a "fine" appointment (i.e. to be well-paid while doing nothing, a view commonly shared in the Soviet country) one had to have a "friend in a court." So, most vacancies at institutes and post-graduate departments were filled by the faculty members' friends and relatives or by freshman instructors from marginal teacher training colleges who were sent to Moscow for further learning in accordance with a special quota. So, despite my desperate efforts, I failed to get a job in the institute.

However, a two-month practice in school in the beginning of the fifth year somewhat changed my attitudes. That time, we dealt with senior classes, the school program itself was more interesting, and we were to independently hold as much as

121

five classes of literature and five of the Russian Language, and organise an obligatory arrangement which would go beyond the frames of the curriculum.

Together with my girlfriend, we arranged a literary soiree. Quite unexpectedly, we found out that we managed to reach the children. Probably, we appeared to be the first teachers who treated them as our full partners, who were interested in what they thought about and felt, what books they liked and why they did like them. That time, it came to my mind that even a Soviet school leaves room for teachers' creativity and self-expression and gives them an option to survive as persons and leave fond memories of themselves. (Running ahead, I would say that I paid a heavy price for this illusion.)

After this experience, I even said good-by to my best-beloved linguistics and changed the topic of my diploma work for a psychology of perception of painting, music and the use of art in and out of literature classes.

After leaving the institute, I found myself at the same secondary school I had graduated from. This meant that I was to work there for three years, having no right to make any shift in my career. Thus, being 21, I became a teacher of the Russian Language and Literature in a secondary school. (Normally, both subjects are taught by the same person from the fourth up to tenth grade.)

Now, perhaps, I am approaching the most crucial episode in the whole story. It was during the first two years at school that largely contributed to my further choice of profession. And, indeed, I have no idea, even cannot imagine, how to explain to those who have grown up in a country with a well-rooted democratic tradition, how the school looked in a totalitarian state. The school administration always "knew the right way to go", where neither teachers, nor students had any rights or options, where some people high-handedly and hard heartedly strengthened themselves at the expense of others, and where a spirit of violence was so strong that it kept corroding students lives even when they left school.

In about a year, I got more or less used to routine functions of a Letters' teacher and of a class master, and did learn everything I was supposed to learn in the Institute. But I understood very soon that <u>what is taught</u> and <u>how it is taught</u> in school is neither helpful, nor interesting for children. I saw that their interests, needs, and the entire life actually had nothing to do with the school where they were to spend much of their time. I felt that I would better try some other ways of teaching.

My acquaintances brought me together with psychologists who were involved in experimental curricula development and working out alternative approaches to teaching. Among them was an outstanding scholar, psychologist, Dr. G. A. Zukerman, who then worked in the Institute for General Pedagogy and Psychology and has later become my partner in developing techniques of the so-called cross-aged learning interaction in the Russian Language classes. The results of our experiments proved to be very promising, and I decided to show them to a person who then headed the Methods of Teaching Russian Department of my former Institute. She appreciated the work and said I could publish it in the professional journal. Moreover, I received an offer to write my doctoral dissertation under supervision of a department's faculty member To do this, I was to go through some formalities, including receiving a recommendation letter from the administration of the school where I worked. It should be mentioned here that a letter of this sort did not commit its authors to anything. It was rather a document confirming "loyalty" of a person who wanted to go in for science.

Nevertheless, as soon as this became known at school, my troubles began. Nobody in our society praised those who stood out a little from the background. I became subject to almost everyday supervision. My superiors carefully examined at what time I came to school and what I did during the classes, whether I strictly followed the obligatory school program (which was quite similar for all schools in the country) or made any step aside from what was prescribed; whether I did check my students' papers after each lesson (note here that I had over 70 students and four or five classes a day) and went out to the school corridor during the breaks to control the children's discipline; what I wrote in my working schedules, and so on, and so on, and so on.

In short, I experienced, to some extent, how the "pressure machine" worked.

Soon after that, the headmistress convened the Teachers' Council, which I, as a teacher, also attended. And I heard something like this: "Prior to inventing your 'new' methods, you were to master to perfection how the elder teachers work. You should do everything what you are told to do by the administration, and if you have enough spare time, we will be pleased to increase your load in school, or, we'll send you to take a course in the Institute of Marxism and Leninism. We do not need researchers, what we do need are good teachers who would devote all their spare time to the school and not to their own career."

I do not know for how long I would withstand such a siege. Luckily, I fell ill, and, under pressure of circumstances (the administration faced a threat of permanently searching for a teacher who could hold my classes while I was ill), the headmistress scrawled her signature under my request to be allowed to leave for another school. So after almost two years of my teacher's career, I, for the first time, enjoyed a right to choose a school myself. Soon, I was lucky to meet a very cultured and democratically-minded headmaster who allowed me to carry out my research in school and wrote a recommendation letter for the Institute.

That's how I "registered" at the Pedagogical Institute as a post-graduate student and, hence, could pass post-graduate exams, namely foreign language, philosophy, and specialty, in my case, education. (Without successfully passing these exams, it is impossible to defend a doctoral dissertation. Parallel to it, I continued to work on my own 'alternative' program in the school.

In about two years, the Sub-department of Methods of Teaching the Russian Language split into two branches, the newly-formed one was to deal with teachers' culture of speech and other problems related to teachers' professional communication activities. I received an offer to take up a job of a laboratory assistant on a part-time basis. I accepted the invitation, but reserved nine academic hours weekly in school for myself. This was done for two reasons. First, I wanted to complete my experimental work. Second I was deeply convinced that a person who is going to train students in teaching methods, shall be in a good form him/ herself. Otherwise, this would be a profanation of teaching.

However, life ruled another way. Rules for entering the daytime post-graduate courses changed, and some people who were to be accepted solely due to their recommendation letters, refused to take the newly-introduced entry exams. Therefore, there were more vacancies than were expected. My chief in the Institute offered me to take a risk. Surprisingly, I got excellent marks for all entry exams, and, four years after leaving the Institute, found myself accepted to a prestigious post graduate course.

The program of three-year-long post-graduate training included four obligatory subjects, that is the information science, pedagogical psychology, educational science in a cultural context, economy and organisation of research. To be positively assessed, one was to present a 24-page written report on each of the disciplines. (Nobody, however, ever read them; just writing a paper was quite enough.)

As for the level of teaching, it left much to be desired. I joined the course in 1988, a year of rapid social change which produced great mental shifts in the public. At the same time, most lecturers still belonged to an old-fashioned communist tradition. Moreover, nobody cared for their doing hack-work, because the disciplines, excluding psychology, had nothing to do with their future career. As for psychology, I began to attend lectures in the Moscow University which were, at least, given by professionals. But on the whole I always lacked time for self-education, given my experiment in school which I continued to carry out.

The next two years should be spent for research work itself, writing two papers for scientific journals (this is a minimum requirement set upon post-graduate students), and participating in obligatory scientific conferences at which one should present his or her original theses.

After granting of a doctoral diploma, one is automatically appointed an instructor in an institution of higher learning. This does not mean, however, that one cannot fill the post without taking a post-graduate course. This is also possible for those who already have a doctoral degree, and in fact, almost 90 percent of faculty in higher school, except freshmen, do have it. Without a doctoral degree, you will not have an opportunity to grow. Sub-departments' faculties have only four types of positions: assistant, senior instructor, assistant professor, and professor. Without a Ph.D. diploma, one can be only an assistant.

In fact, there are cases when a post-graduate student cannot defend his or her thesis immediately after completing the course scientific councils which are to approve the thesis before granting a doctoral degree, used to meet only once per month. Sometimes, the defence of a thesis can be delayed for as much as six months solely for this reason.

What is more, women have a strange habit of giving birth to children. This typically happens quite at the wrong time and this was purely my case. Because of time shortage I failed to defend before the birth of my daughter and am supposed to do it this year.

Pitifully, I had only a year's experience of teaching in a higher school. My job functions as of an assistant included holding seminars with students (all the topics were to coincide with the plan designed by the faculty staff), supervise over students' practice in school (this meant weekly attending classes they held), and passing students and applicants in the required subjects. The overall load totaled to 800 academic hours a year.

However, a year was quite enough to make me understand that the years of reform failed to result in diminishing the scope of mores and abundance in training of future teachers. In the process of teaching, we still keep ignoring all what makes up the very heart of teachers' profession. We never pay attention to developing an ability to organise the classroom activities, as well as to making our lessons actually interesting. In short, we do not teach educational technologies.

However, we have even more than enough academic freedom in our higher school. The only two things we are obliged to do are to follow the general line of a learning course and to discuss a core content specified in the faculty's plan with several groups of trainees. What else you will do with your students depends on your own opinion and imagination.

Actually, I am even glad that now I am not conducting classes. This enables me to have a look round simply to study teacher training materials which come from abroad. (Formerly we had no access to this information.) I would like to learn what and how future teachers are taught in other countries, especially in the United States, where the education seems to have more rational grounds and is more practice-oriented.

It seems to me that American educational technologies, if implanted in the Russian soil, could result in constructive and viable developments. I would like to hope that I will have a chance to put them into practice.

Though I am still connected with education field and supervising a project in one of Moscow Schools, I am no longer a university teacher. There have been difficult times for Russian high school and science in general. So, after I've received a Ph.D. in Education, I will accept a job offer from the Procter & Gamble Company to become their Human Resources Specialist. My new assignment is closely connected with my professional background: I am dealing with interviewing people and training personnel. Nevertheless, it is not teaching of teachers. I continue as a volunteer on a project at school with two teachers.

I began my story from the point that I had become an instructor in a teacher training institution absolutely by chance. But now, it came to my mind that life itself is so strange that many things which seemed occasional at a first glance, are in fact duly predetermined. Probably, a human being simply cannot judge upon his or her life without reservations. Anyway, I tried to be honest and frank. The rest is up to the reader.

My "Crash-Landing" Into Teaching And Teacher Education

Bill Fraser
South Africa

I was born in 1949, and am currently professor and Head of the Department of Didactics, Faculty of Education, University of Pretoria. I taught biology for ten years at the high school level, spent five years with the Human Sciences Research Council (HSRC) in test construction and taught biology at Vista University. I was appointed as a senior lecturer at UNISA in 1987, promoted to associate professor in 1989, and appointed full professor in 1994. In 1997 I accepted the position at the University of Pretoria.

General Orientation

Teaching and teacher education in the Republic of South Africa had always been a highly controversial and segregated issue, mainly because of prior "Apartheid" governments' policy that education should be regarded as an "own affair," and which also had to be treated as such by the different racial and cultural "groups" which form part of the diverse and culturally rich population. Although my "story" does share many commonalties with those of other colleagues in teacher training in South Africa, it would be wrong to read it as the only, or even, the common approach to teacher training in this country. Under the "old" dispensation, education was served by approximately ten education departments (including the departments of the so-called "independent states" and "homelands") within the boundaries of the RSA, conducting their own teacher training courses and prescribing their own entry qualifications. This excluded the training programmes of the twenty universities who have to educate teachers according to national criteria. The structure changed significantly following the country's first democratic general election in 1994.

Another issue which has to be raised is the philosophical foundations from which teacher training has been conducted in this country. The predominantly Afrikaans-speaking universities and colleges adhered to a more conservative educational philosophy-- conservative in the sense that teacher training at these institutions was mostly rooted in the much criticized CNE or Christian National Education, while most of the English speaking institutions followed a core liberal and even liberating approach in their teaching.

The title of my story depicts the general perception of teaching and teacher training in South Africa in the early seventies. Many teachers and teacher trainers "landed" in education mainly because of the limited opportunities other careers had to offer at that time, and of their own doing. The government of the time placed a high premium on teacher education, and bursaries to attend teacher training institutions were relatively freely available. When I left high school, I shared with many other students similar problems which placed university or college education out of reach of many of these students: average matric passes with relatively low marks, and matriculating from a school with an average social standing in the community.

The easiest way of getting into a university or college, was by means of a bursary awarded by one of the provincial administrations which administered education in each of the four provinces of the Republic of South Africa. At that time, education departments experienced a shortage of especially biology, physical science, and mathematics teachers, which to a certain extent, is still presently experienced in South Africa. National criteria regarding teacher qualifications offered a few possibilities to prospective student teachers: a two year Primary Education Certificate and a three year Primary Education Diploma for students interested in a primary school career, a Secondary Education Certificate or Diploma (also a three year course) for high school teachers, and a four year Higher Education Diploma for high school teachers. Universities offered various combinations such as the classical B. Prim Ed. for primary school teachers, an independent bachelor's degree followed by a Higher Education Diploma (3 + 1), or a combined teaching qualification such as a four year B.A. Ed., B.Sc. Ed. or B.Com. Ed. I enrolled for a B.Sc. degree with majors in botany and zoology, and a simultaneous higher education diploma, the 3 + 1 combination (a bachelor's degree offering at least two school subjects and a professional higher education diploma) at that time. I graduated in 1973 and began a teaching career at a small country high school with a staff of 18 with 350 students. To be competitive with the much larger high schools in the bigger towns and cities, most of the subjects listed in the normal school curriculum were also offered by these smaller schools with the much smaller staff. Although qualified to teach only biology and geography, I also had to teach general science, biblical instruction, geography, mathematics, and history at the elementary level. Coaching also took much of my time. I coached hockey (which I enjoyed), and did some cross-country and middle distances training during the summer months. In many of the schools where I taught, a good performance by the school teams in any of the national sporting activities was regarded as an absolute necessity. This ensured a high social standing in the community and to many parents, became a criterion to distinguish between a "good" and a "better" school. Many teachers, therefore, took up coaching by attending one of the many coaching clinics offered by the sporting bodies. A successful coaching career not only guaranteed promotion, but also ensured a teaching post at one of the "better" schools.

Residence in the boys' hostel offered cheap boarding and lodging but with an additional responsibility-- that of house master! This initiation into the realities of teaching, as well as the rigid, highly disciplined and very authoritative schooling and educational system, often contributed to the fact that many teachers left the teaching profession when alternative attractive options became available. Even to this day, many teachers enroll for post-graduate courses with the sole intention of working themselves gradually out of classroom teaching!

Professional Development

Very few teachers enrolled for post-graduate courses with the sole intention of becoming teacher educators. An additional qualification brought a teacher within range of promotion, as well as a salary increase which was automatically linked to higher qualification. When I applied for the post of teacher educator for the first time, teacher training institutions at that stage expected of applicants to be in possession of an honours degree (which could have been an honours degree in a school subject such as botany), or a post-graduate B.Ed. degree which entitled a

131

person to teach the pedagogical subjects such as history of education, comparative education, method, didactics, educational psychology and educational administration and management. Better qualifications also brought teachers within range of various teaching, research, or administrative posts. Teachers with experience were absorbed by research institutions, support services, subject advisory services, counselling departments, curriculum development units, and teacher training institutions.

Teachers of the natural sciences found and still find difficulty in enrolling in a post-graduate degree in botany, zoology, chemistry, physics, or geography due to the compulsory practical work which forms part of these courses and therefore made attendance difficult. A B.Ed. (post-graduate), therefore, became my only option which I completed in 1979 through the University of South Africa (UNISA), a distance teaching institution which acted as the examination body for the fairly young university colleges in the early fifties. A master's degree in the subject didactics of biology followed suit in 1983. By the end of 1986 I had also completed my doctoral studies through UNISA.

I left the high school where I had been teaching biology for approximately three years, and took up a position as test developer with the Human Sciences Research Council (HSRC), a body similar to that of ACER, TCA, and ETS. It was here where I experienced my first contact with the education of teachers, as we had to train teachers in item writing and test construction.

My Appointment As Teacher Educator

Similar to many other developing countries, the majority teachers in this country are under qualified in terms of a good teaching certificate, diploma or degree. Many are poorly equipped to teach the more demanding subjects such as mathematics, accounting, and physical science, as many of them offered the "easier" options such as biblical studies, library science, a home language, or an indigenous language during their initial training. Many teachers, therefore, enroll at distance teaching institutions to upgrade their teaching qualifications. The College of Education of South Africa, Vista University's Further Training Campus, and the University of South Africa for many years remained the only three institutions offering inservice training to teachers at a distance in the immediate greater Pretoria area.

My first appointment as teacher educator came as lecturer at Vista University's Further Training Campus (currently known as VUDEC), and a year thereafter as senior lecturer in the Department of Didactics, Faculty of Education at the University of South Africa. Since 1997 I have been Head of the Department of Didactics at the University of Pretoria.

My Tasks As Teacher Educator

One would normally find teacher educators becoming involved mainly with two aspects or components of teacher training--the one being a pedagogical subject such as general didactics (teaching science), history or education, philosophy of education, or educational psychology, and the other being the specific subject didactics of the school subject the student teacher will eventually be teaching after completing his or her postgraduate teacher diploma. But the task of teacher educators at most Southern African universities stretches beyond the education of student teachers in the different academic and professional subjects. Universities and colleges expect teacher educators to become involved with research in the educators' fields of specialization, and to commit themselves to some form of community service, such as literacy programmes. There are many reasons why scientists are encouraged to report their findings. In South Africa research outputs of universities are subsidized by the state and the funds generated by teaching departments are used to fund further research. Local communities could also acquire the professional skills of teachers, educators, and subject specialists. In a developing country there are ample opportunities for teacher educators to become involved with such community programmes and projects. Many subject specialists are involved with the teaching of school subjects to disadvantaged pupils at secondary level. I, myself, had been involved with the setting of examination papers and the marking and moderation of such scripts for many years. Many daily newspapers publish hints on the writing of the different external examinations towards the end of the year, and many of us have also been involved with the writing of such articles.

I was course coordinator for the didactics component of the Education I course, as well as for the subject didactics of biology, one of the subjects which I taught at high school. During 1993, approximately 10,000 students enrolled for Education I, while only a limited number of 20 students wrote the final postgraduate examination in the subject didactics of biology. One must remember that, at the University of South Africa, the Education course is not only offered as an option to practising or prospective teachers (although close to 90% of the students who enrolled for the course in the past had always been under qualified and wished to

133

upgrade their qualifications) but also to students who are directly or indirectly involved with the teaching and instruction (training) of staff.

One of my tasks was to offer discussion classes to our students in a number of subjects. These discussion classes were held at many of the centres especially developed for the distance learners in the major cities in South Africa. I also had to offer so-called day seminars for our postgraduate subject didactics students at UNISA's main campus in Pretoria.

Although we didn't personally go out to assess the performance of our many student teachers during teaching practice, students were assessed by the senior teachers and headmasters of the different schools where our students preferred to do the compulsory teaching practice of ten weeks at a school of their choice. During this period of time they had to present twenty lessons which were then assessed by the attending senior teacher. The workbooks in which lessons have been set out, were then returned to us for evaluation.

Much of our time was taken up by the preparation and production of tutorial material which was mailed to all students with the commencement of the academic year. We also did a lot of writing. I completed a revision of our general didactics textbook, and published a biology subject didactics textbook.

Future Perspectives

I have already referred to our country's first democratic elections which took take place on the 27th of April 1994. The result of this election has had a tremendous influence on education in the country. With more than five million children who still have to enter primary school within the next few years, one could only speculate which measures will have to be considered to accommodate the entire pupil population in the near future.

Politicians are already considering the retraining of thousands of teachers who teach in the more than 30,000 schools in South Africa. This will place a tremendous task on the shoulders of educators in the distance teaching institutions who could expect to be requested to do the training.

However, the restructuring of education in South Africa has also brought along a number of dilemmas not previous experienced in the country. The restructuring of a single national education department, as well as the stretching of budgets, are contributing to the closing down of many teacher education colleges, the adoption of so-called "right sizing" principles in state schools, and the retrenchment of thousands of teachers in a country where the skills and expertise of well-educated teachers are so much needed.

Teaching and teacher training are moving towards an interesting era in this southern tip of Africa, and I can only conclude by saying that I am proud and happy to be part of the teacher training team!

A Curriculum Vitae Of A Teacher Educator

Walter Furrer
Switzerland

My name is Walter Furrer. I born in 1945 and I have been working since 1972 in teacher education. Today I am director of the *Seminar fur Padagogische Grundausbildung* in Zurich, Switzerland. Our Teacher Training College offers a two semesters course the purpose of which is to introduce high school graduates into the profession of a teacher. During their studies at the *Seminar fur Padagogische Grundausbildung* the students decide whether to become a primary or a secondary school teacher. Depending on this decision they will later complete their studies at a more specialized teacher training college respectively. As director I am not so much involved into teaching anymore. It is only three lessons a week I am still teaching myself. Most of my time is spent on personnel management, administration, conception and on projects involving other teacher training colleges within the canton of Zurich or even on a national level. Of course it has not been like this all the time. I used to commit all my time and all my efforts to training teachers. How I became a teacher trainer? This is my story:

I never intended to become a teacher trainer. To become a teacher even had not been one of my primary goals by any means. The parents of my classmates were lawyers or businessmen and earned a lot more than my own father did, who was-- guess what--a teacher himself. The fact that none of them tried to hide their better economical status made me think that becoming a teacher was not exactly the career to choose. But nevertheless I entered professional life as a primary teacher. I think

137

there were three reasons. First of all: The closest school that provided higher education was a teacher training college. Second: My father was very happy with his job. He never complained about going to work and mentioned over and over that he would choose the same profession again. Third: I always liked working with children and teenagers. As soon as I had gotten the first impressions of a teacher's professional life at the teacher training college I had no doubts about my aims any more.

Having graduated from the teacher training college as a primary teacher I was trusted with the teaching of a seventh level (secondary level) class. At this time there was a serious lack of teachers on this level. That is the reason why I had to teach some thirteen students in *all* subjects including subjects such as French, metal handicrafts and gymnasium without having been trained really for this specific task myself. I still keep asking myself how I managed this difficult situation. Most of my students were tired of school, many of them already had to repeat classes and others were in the middle of a heavy puberty crisis. In spite of all this my first year of teaching passed without any greater accidents. I was now to decide whether trying to find a job as a primary teacher somewhere or maybe rather going back to the teacher training college to get a diploma for teaching on the secondary level as well. A phenomenon completely new to myself finally made the decision: I was hungry to learn. Having tried to pass over knowledge for a whole year I just could not believe that I myself was not to learn anymore. I then inscribed at the University of Zurich to study history, geography and high school didactics. My new goal: high school history and geography teacher.

In the course of my studies at the University of Zurich having a teaching diploma proved very advantageous for me. I had various opportunities to help out at different high schools in the area and gain more and more teaching experience this way. Of course this was a most welcomed opportunity to earn some money for a living as well.

After five years at the university I finally got my master's and two years later my doctorate and I was ready to pass my new knowledge to others. Just at this time, however, another most important event demanded all my attention: My wife, who is a primary school teacher herself, gave birth to our eldest son. The class she was teaching was orphaned due to this event and needed another teacher right away. I therefore took over the teaching of her class and completed their course until the end of the school year in April. The children did not have many difficulties with the change: Instead of Mrs. Furrer it was Mr. Furrer that taught them.

Besides teaching my wife's class, I spent a lot of time looking for a job. This was a rather difficult and time consuming task since there was no need for history or geography teachers whatsoever. I finally managed to get part time employment at three different high schools which made me believe I cleared the roads for a future career as a high school teacher.

At the school where I taught my wife's class I accidentally met one of my former teachers at the teacher training center. He remembered me and asked about what I had been doing after leaving the center. Upon the description of my professional career he suggested talking to his director who was looking for someone teaching subject didactics in history and geography at the teacher training center. In Switzerland there was no specific training for this task that is why they had always employed primary school teachers with an additional university degree in these subjects.

I liked the thought of having a try as a teacher trainer. So I introduced myself to the director of the teacher training center and was promptly rewarded with the mandate to teach two lessons of subject didactics a week.

So I started with teaching at three high schools as a history and geography teacher and as a teacher for subject didactics at the training center in spring. This phase of my career was a constant struggle for survival. I did not have any experience in teaching at a high school yet but at least I had been trained for that task. Both history and geography however are subjects that require an immense amount of work to seriously prepare lessons for. To teach didactics for these two subjects was almost impossible because my background was limited. My colleagues at the teacher training center however were very helpful and provided me with material and tips. In spite of their readily offered help I think my subject didactics course was not a great success. Sometimes I hoped never to meet again those students I had tried to teach there. Such was my bad conscience not having been able to provide them with a satisfactory education. Of course I have met quite a lot of them again but their reactions have shown me that most of them have forgiven me due to the fact that I was still rather young (27 years) for such a task.

Only a semester after I had started teaching at the teacher training center I had to decide whether to concentrate on working as a teacher trainer or as a high school teacher, since a full time job for a teacher trainer was vacant at the center. In spite of all the problems I liked working with adult students a lot. Moreover, I had confidence in becoming a quite all right subjects didactics teacher after these rather difficult beginnings. I applied for the job and was, to my utter surprise, voted to be the youngest member of the teaching staff.

This was the decision, I now was a teacher trainer. I gave up my engagement at the high schools and committed myself wholly to my autodidactic education as a subject didactics teacher. I worked through all the available literature as fast as possible and tested my teaching methods in cooperation with former primary school teacher friends. Besides I was to teach teaching skills and practical teaching. Thanks to the cooperation with my colleagues I managed to work out an acceptable teaching programme in above subjects after a few years.

After seven years of working as a teacher trainer I was elected deputy-director and after another eight years director. This also led to my being a member in a national committee that consists of experts in teacher training and has to discuss basic questions related to teacher training that are of a nation wide, not just a cantonal interest. Remembering the problems I had as a newcomer to teaching subject didactics I suggested during one of the meetings of this committee that the training for subject didactics teacher should be institutionalized. Upon this suggestion a special committee was formed to study this problem. As president of this committee I am proud that the government decided to introduce a specialized institute for the training of subject didactics teachers until 1995. My professional career is typical of the way how most of my Swiss colleagues became teacher educators. The same thing is true for directors of teacher training colleges. It is a career marked by autodidactic learning and learning by doing, a career where there are no shortcuts but a lot of obstacles and detours. Even now as a TTC-director I am still trying to solve some of the same basic problems I used to work on when I was a teacher for subject didactics. The most urgent of these questions I would like to list below.

- What learning processes have to be experienced by teacher students in the course of their basic training so that it is guaranteed that they will later be able to succeed in their professional activities? Teacher training as a prophylactic instrument.
- How can we better link theory and practice?

140

-How can we motivate the future teaching staff to cooperate even more intensively?

- How can we promote independent learning?

- How can we motivate the right young people to become teachers?

- How can we improve aptitude tests?

I am afraid not having been able to find the final answers to above questions even after over 26 years of experience in teacher training. But I have not abandoned hope.

Teacher Educators In Turkey

Kadir Dalgiç
Turkey

Many children between the ages of eight and twelve want to become doctors, engineers, or lawyers when they grow up, but few of them are interested in teaching. Why do those children have that kind of tendency not to become teachers? The reality is that their families, relatives, and environment have a strong influence on them considering the economical conditions, the values of the community and a high standard of living in the society.

I was born in Corum in 1944. As usual, I began my education when I was seven years old. After my elementary and high school education, I took the examinations of Gazi Teacher Training Institute in Ankara. During that time it was a boarding institute, and now it is Gazi Faculty of Education. I graduated from Gazi Teacher Training Institute in 1968. Since then I have been working as a teacher of English.

In 1968, I began teaching in Konya Anatolian High School, I worked there for four years. In 1972 I was assigned to Izmir Anatolian High School. Anatolian High Schools are schools where the students study and learn a foreign language. Some of the subjects are taught through the language students are studying. Although, some subjects such as Turkish, national history, geography, and civic duty are taught in Turkish. English is studied in many of Anatolian High Schools. French and German are also available in some Anatolian schools.

When I began teaching, I was very young and inexperienced. But I was full of energy, and I was willing to teach many things to my students. I was doing my best to be successful for my students.

Anatolian High School graduates are successful students at universities. My purpose was to influence them to become teachers. Unfortunately they often chose other careers because these led to higher status better salary, and fringe benefits.

In 1976, I was assigned to Higher School of Foreign Languages. This school provides two years of education after high school and they are similar to colleges in the United States and Polytechnic schools in the United Kingdom. In 1982, faculties of education joined the Higher Schools of Foreign Languages. Since then I have been working at Buca Faculty of Education in the English Department.

In my faculty, we educate teacher trainees. Students come from different high schools and from different towns and cities. They all have different backgrounds.

In my country, students begin their elementary school education at the age of six or seven. They have five years of education. After elementary school education, students take an examination to attend Anatolian High Schools. The students who don't wish to take the examinations, and the ones who do not pass the examinations attend public secondary schools. The high school course of study is three years (students study in secondary schools for three years and high school is another three years). On the other hand, students who pass the examinations attend Anatolian High Schools where they study a foreign language in the preparatory class for a year. If the students successfully pass the examinations at the end of the year, they become the first year students and stay in schools for six years. Thus Anatolian High Schools consist of seven years, one year more than public high schools. (Students who attend secondary and high schools have a six year curriculum.) There are also private high schools similar to Anatolian High Schools. Private high school students pay tuition. The private high schools provide either preparatory classes or extra foreign language instruction.

After secondary school education, some students attend State Technical High Schools. The technical schools are different from public high schools and Anatolian High Schools. They provide specific curricula for technical training such as trade and tourism courses.

All high school graduates qualify to take entrance examinations for the universities. Once the students pass the examinations, they indicate which

144

universities and departments they wish to attend. Students then take a second university examination. Based on their scores, students are placed at different universities and their respective departments by the Institute of High Education. Students who do not pass the examinations may retake them the next year.

A student who wants to become a teacher may or may not get the opportunity to study at a university. As student can make up to eight choices for different universities and their departments. The first choice can be at a university with a department of education. If the student's score is not high enough the university will not accept the student. Students are in competition for the university of their choice. Sometimes a student may only qualify for the seventh or eighth choice. Students who do not get accepted at universities with teacher preparation programs cannot become teachers. And, it is not possible to become a teacher educator unless one has been a teacher.

At the first look, it may appear that acceptance to a teacher preparation program at a university of choice is a matter of chance or luck, however, the student's score on the second examination is what determines where the Institute of High Education will place the student.

Students in the faculties of education come from different high schools and they have been placed based on their test scores. This means the abilities and competence of students are not the same (some come from the Anatolian high Schools, others come from the three year high schools), but after four years of education they become teachers. Until 1982 there were Teacher Training Institutions. Teachers were educated in those institutions. In 1982 The Institute of Higher Education was founded, and Teacher Training Institutions were reorganized as Faculties of Education. Thus these faculties are responsible for training teachers and teacher educators. The curriculum and courses of study were revised to meet the needs of the country, and they are still under review.

In the faculties, teacher educators are supposed to participate in many activities, both academic and non academic. These activities include doing research, making speeches, attending conferences, seminars, panels. Teacher educators are expected to write essays and/or books in their areas of expertise. Sight-seeing tours, tea parties, and other social activities for good relationship among the students, and sports activities and so on are arranged to be familiar with the students. The goal is to create a family relationship between faculty and students.

Teacher educators also lead teacher trainees to form positive attitudes toward the teaching profession, to love human beings, to like students, and to behave kindly to others. Being patient, tolerable, understanding, polite, honest, and generous are the virtues of this career. Without those values, many things which are done by spending money and time to train and educate teacher educators won't be much use for the students and the country. Unless more students benefit their teachers it seems impossible for contemporary education to advance. Keeping all of this in mind, teacher educators do their best to be helpful for teacher trainees. You may give a lot of knowledge to students, you may be the best guide for them, but unless you train and educate them for future, I believe you are not an effective educator. As teacher educators, we always think of these values. If we do not forget them, and work as hard as we can, we can get the fruits of these values.

Generally, students begin their university education when they are between the ages of eighteen or twenty-two. After registration, they continue their education for four years. In the language departments, there are preparatory classes. After registration students are given a placement test. The students who are not successful in the test attend a preparatory class for a year, thus their university education lasts five years.

I teach grammar and methodology (how to teach English to Turkish students). Teaching grammar is thought to be the most boring class. The purpose of teaching grammar should be the oral use of the learned patterns for effective communication, and learners should use those patterns in their writing activities. In my methodology class, I try to do my best to be a good model for my students. As it is known, students are good judges. They can criticize you better than an inspector can. Through their criticism, a teacher can identify weak and strong points of a teaching techniques. I give them opportunities to teach a subject matter. They prepare their lessons, and present them in front of their peers. After a presentation, teacher trainees begin their criticisms of the lesson. By means of those criticisms both the students and I understand what was wrong and what was right about the lesson. I take my students to the public secondary and high schools to observe students and teachers. They observe and analyze classroom activities. My students also do practice teaching in schools, and talk to the class teachers who evaluate their practice teaching. To become an effective teacher, it is important to understand both the theory and application of teaching techniques. To become an effective teacher is

146

not easy. The success of a course depends on not only the behavior of the teacher but also on the qualifications of the teacher. Therefore, students are required to learn psychology, child psychology guidelines, grading and evaluation, beginning of educational science, educational technology and philosophy.

In the different departments of the faculties of education, all students take these lessons, and branch lessons. In addition, students have laboratory experiences in each of these departments. After four years of study students receive their diplomas.

After graduation teacher candidates who want to become teachers, fill out application forms and send them to the Ministry of Education. These applications are evaluated by the Ministry of Education, based on the needs of the country, the candidates are assigned to different schools--elementary, secondary and high schools--in Turkey.

The graduates of faculties of education can work as teachers in elementary, secondary and high schools. These teachers are able to do post graduate studies. If they want to continue their studies, they have to apply for post graduate studies at any of the universities in the country. They may also do their post graduate studies in any foreign countries. According to their areas of expertise, when their applications are accepted, they must take two examinations. One of them is a foreign language examination, and the other one is their speciality examination. If they pass those two examinations, they begin their studies at the universities. They have a twelve hour lesson or a sixteen hour lesson load a week during the academic year. At the end of the academic year student take examinations. If they pass the examinations, they begin to prepare their theses under the supervision of a professor or an associate professor. When their theses are accepted and signed, they receive their M.A. degrees. It takes two or three years to get a M.A. degree. Those who receive an M.A. can take examinations to become research assistants. The successful candidates are assigned as research assistants and they begin to work in the faculties. If we think of time, we can say that a person may become a research assistant within nineteen or twenty years, having attended elementary, secondary, high school, university, and doing post graduate study.

Research assistants do not teach lessons and they do not give lectures. They observe the academic and non academic activities, and prepare their doctorate theses under the supervision of professors or associate professors. When their studies and theses are approved and accepted by the professors and associate professors, the candidates receive their Ph.D. degrees. It takes four or five years to complete a doctoral thesis. At this time the graduate can begin to teach and give lectures. They also continue their study, write essays or books. Their works are evaluated by professors and associate professors. When their works are judged to be of quality, they become assistant associate professors. It takes three, four, or five years to become an assistant associate professor. Teacher educators work as assistant associate professors before they become associate professors.

Assistant associate professors write essays and books. The professors check their works. When they are accepted, they become associate professors. Associate professors continue to study for at least five years. After this period of time their works are evaluated by the committee of professors. When their works are approved, they become professors. The teaching staff consists of professors, associate professors, assistant associate professors, and lecturers in the faculties of education. These people are teacher educators; they prepare teachers and teacher educators. It is also possible for the graduates of other faculties to do post graduate studies in the faculties of education. They study for a long time, prepare their theses, get their M.A. and Ph.D. degrees as I have already explained above.

The Ministry of Education and the Institute of Higher Education have been studying a new project since 1995. The aim of the project is to educate and train teacher trainees better than before and to equip them with the knowledge which will be necessary in the twenty-first century. A lot of universitites have been interesteed in the project, and professors, specialists, and teachers have been working on it. The supervisors from the British Council and funds from The World Bank have been suporting the project. We hope it will be a success and will help the educational system in our country.

Teaching is one of the most difficult jobs in the world. A person may become a professional in any job or work, but to become an effective teacher is a more complex process.

One may ask why. Millions of students in a country have different habits, ideas, or thoughts about the same topic, and they show different behavior and attitudes toward their friends, people, and teachers around them. Culture, region, customs, religion, etc. are all important factors in the training and preparation of teachers and teacher educators. Teachers and teacher educators come face to face with human beings. When we are able to understand with each other, we can continue teaching. When there is no communication between the teachers and the students, a lot of problems will occur, and the prevention of them will be rather difficult.

Teachers and teacher educators and students are always in a place called "school" or "university." They are the members of the same family. Teacher educators should be trained and educated well, should be prepared psychologically, and should understand the conditions, circumstances, and the needs of the country. To be effective, they must treat each other with respect.

We are in the space era, and everything in the world is changing rapidly. No one denies there won't be new development for human beings in the world in the twenty first century. What causes civilisation to make progress? When do people use the new development for the use of humanity? The answer lies in the education process.

The Making of an American Teacher Educator

William Scott Thomson
United States of America

My name is William Scott Thomson. I was born in Providence, Rhode Island in 1950, and lived for 33 years in Maryland and Florida before moving to North Carolina where I currently work and live. I am an Associate Professor in the Department of Elementary and Middle Grades Education in the School of Education at East Carolina University (located in the eastern part of North Carolina, about midway up the east coast of the United States). Based upon numbers of programs and student enrollment, East Carolina University has the largest School of Education in the state of North Carolina, and its annual production of teaching candidates ranks it about fifteenth in size when compared to other similar schools of education across the United States. It is the fourth largest preparer of minority teachers in the United States of America.

I entered the teaching profession in 1976 (when I was 26), and was an elementary school teacher for about seven and half years prior to becoming a professor. I have been a teacher educator for twelve years. While I have periodically supplemented my income in a variety of ways, and even entertained the notion of leaving the profession, I have always been, and likely I will always be, a teacher. The path that I followed to reach my current position is not entirely typical of the process that many Americans might complete in order to become a professor, and specifically to become a teacher educator.

151

When I began my teaching career in 1976, I came to teaching via a rather circuitous route. In 1968 I dropped out of high school, which precluded my going on to attend the university or college as others might do. I worked at a series of menial jobs before realizing my error in deciding to leave school early. After work, in the evenings, I began attending adult education classes, completing my high school education in 1969. I went on to attend junior college for two years, and upon graduation, continued my bachelor's degree studies at a regional upper-division university. I was initially undecided as to my major course of study, but after taking a diverse array of courses in the humanities, I realized that I was more interested in how I was being taught--in how learners learn--than in the content itself. I took some courses in education, and eventually settled on elementary education, largely due to my favorable methods-course experiences with children in the schools. I was convinced that teaching in an elementary school would be a rewarding career.

As an elementary school teacher, I taught a variety of different grades in two different school systems. For most of my public school teaching career I served in a small, rural district in Florida, teaching all of the subjects to a sixth grade class in a regional school which enrolled grades K-12. This region, located in the "panhandle" of the state, was so sparsely populated that for several years, in addition to my regular teaching duties, I drove a school bus in a fifty-mile circuit to pick up the children and to deliver them home again.

In those days, before the advent of a state mandated curriculum, teachers were very active in curriculum design, and so, along with many other teachers, I spent several summers revising and redesigning the elementary curriculum for my district. As I became progressively more skilled as a teacher, I was asked to participate in the supervision and training of beginning teachers. This participation ultimately resulted in my being trained by the state in what was then an emerging educational concept--viewing teaching as a science, which in turn gave birth to the ideal of teaching effectiveness.

When I was not teaching I served my school in a variety of extracurricular roles. This is typical for teachers everywhere, but it is particularly important in a rural setting where adult volunteers make the difference between offering or not offering certain sports or activities. I was the announcer at the high school football games, drove the bus that transported the high school basketball team, and served as advisor to the cheerleading team. Any carnival, fair, or school-based activity generally had my support and made use of my energy. It was personally important for me that a sufficient number of quality extracurricular programs were available for the children.

Becoming active in the local teachers association, I learned to represent the teachers' grievances, and to negotiate their salaries and working conditions for them, eventually becoming president of the association. In order to renew my teaching license, I enrolled in graduate courses with the intention of ultimately becoming a school administrator. From 1977 to 1981, I amassed a considerable number of semester hours by attending a graduate school part-time, taking one new course each succeeding semester. Over the years my administrative intentions were realized: I served as a grade-level chairman, as chairman of the intermediate school, and finally in 1981 as an administrative assistant to the principal. I left the public school system in 1982 to pursue full-time graduate studies at a local university, principally because administrators were required to possess a master's degree and there was a residency requirement that I attend full-time two consecutive semesters in order to complete my degree.

It was during my master's degree studies (in social studies education) that I began to think about becoming a professor. Like most people outside of the academy, I had little understanding of the requirements involved, or of the process one must undertake in order to compete for a college or university position. I have since served on many search committees and have developed a clear profile of the average prospective candidate. Most elementary teacher education positions call for an individual who has, at minimum, three years of public school teaching experience in the appropriate specialty area. As an example, I was hired to teach methods courses so those years spent planning, teaching, and supervising children gave me both practical experience to which I could refer and a degree of credibility in the students' eyes. Typically a professor in teacher education has at least three degrees. Many colleges and universities now require that a professor be eligible for and/or hold a current teacher's license in a valid specialty area. Most teacher educators also have a content area in which they specialize. Almost all professors hold a doctorate in their field. Most universities and colleges will no longer consider a candidate for a position who is not close to his or her dissertation defense at the time of the interview. While those who do not possess

153

the doctorate may be hired, they are usually not placed in a tenure-track position, and so they are limited to a fixed period of annual employment.

I have a Bachelor of Arts degree in Elementary Education, which qualified me to become initially licensed and to gain entry into the teaching field. My Master of Science degree in Social Studies Education allows me to teach a social studies content area methods course, and my Doctor of Philosophy in Elementary Education (with a cognate area in statistics) entitles me to teach in my specialty area at the university and also qualifies me to conduct research. These credentials also allow me to guide students through graduate work at the master's degree and doctoral degree level. At my institution it is considered a privilege to be a member of the graduate level faculty. Members of the graduate faculty must, in addition to possessing appropriate degrees and credentials, demonstrate their abilities to conduct ongoing research and to publish in appropriate journals. Only after they have done these things may they apply and be elected to the graduate faculty.

Currently, I teach juniors, seniors, and master's degree students enrolled in courses in curriculum theory and both general and content specific methods of teaching. The junior level undergraduate theory class on elementary curriculum helps these prospective elementary school teachers understand how schools operate and how disciplinary knowledge is communicated to the children both within and across the grade levels. The junior-level general methods course explains the lesson planning process, and assists the students in developing skills for making planning decisions and acting out daily, weekly, and semester long plans. All of the undergraduate teacher education classes at ECU are coupled with field-based clinical experiences, so as students learn theory at the university, they can implement that theory and refine their practice in a public school setting. University assignments are acted out in local school classroom settings with elementary school children. I also teach a senior-level social studies methods course. Somewhat similar to the general methods course in its structure, the social etudes methods course assists students in communicating social studies knowledge gained in their college level arts and sciences courses to elementary children in an active rather than passive manner, providing the children with many hands-on and interactive activities.

At the graduate level my department offers a Master of Arts in Education degree (M.A.Ed.). I direct the graduate program and teach graduate courses in both curriculum theory and advanced social studies methods. Each of these courses are designed to expand and enhance basic knowledge gained by the students at the undergraduate level. The majority of the students in these courses are practicing teachers who have come to graduate school to gain a more comprehensive understanding of the environment in which they work and to improve their teaching practices.

As a professor at East Carolina University, I am expected to be an effective teacher (assessed each semester by a survey given to my students); to conduct research and publish in refereed journals (those which send out potential manuscripts to be peer-evaluated by other professionals in the field)--preferably those with a national readership--and present the results; and to provide service to my institution and the surrounding education community. I have elected to have my yearly evaluations weighted equally at 33% in each of these activities. In addition to these duties, I edit the *North Carolina Journal of Teacher Education,* a responsibility for which I am released from teaching one of the classes to which I would normally be assigned. At ECU a normal teaching load is considered to be four 3-semester-hour (s.h.) courses per semester, however, I am now teaching only two (5 s.h. and 3 s.h.), for a total of eight semester hours; still, about 40% of my time is invested in teaching. Another 25% is spent administratively assisting the department chair.

Since becoming a professor I have published, on average, one or two articles a year in state, regional and national journals. In 1992, with a colleague, I published an edited book. In 1992, with a colleague I contributed a chapter in the United Nations Curriculum Guide. I make an average of two to three presentations a year at state, regional and national meetings of professional organizations affiliated to my profession. I am encouraged to solicit grant-supported research. Most recently I have been engaged in externally funded research, conducting collaborative research with a local school system. Research, publishing, and presenting takes up 10% of my time, however, my teaching focus and research agenda overlap considerably.

On campus I serve on a minimum of three university committees (another 10%), one each at the department, school, and university level. Within the department in which I serve, I am assigned academic advisement responsibility for thirty to fifty undergraduate and graduate students (10%). I hold an office in a national teacher organization, the Association of Teacher Educators, and I serve on one of its committees. While such national activity is very much endorsed by my institution, it is an individual investment in terms of both time (5%) and money. At the local level

I support the regional educational community by working with high school students at the High School Quiz Bowl, and provide consulting services to the local school system at the elementary level when requested.

Emerging technology is reshaping how we teach and how we visualize teaching. In contrast to previous years, the presence of computer workstations in our offices is now the norm rather than the exception. Teacher educators are being asked to put aside their pencils and pens and to take up the mouse and the keypad. We are now attempting to teach preservice teachers to make use of technologies that we ourselves never experienced in our teaching careers. Increasingly we are being asked to collaborate with public school systems in developing new teacher education training models. More and more candidates for certification are coming to us through irregular paths--non-traditional students who possess degrees and have prior experience in other vocations. Public school systems are hiring more of these candidates and then remanding them to us for certification only. These trends, and others, are certainly causing us to reconceptualize our notions of our own roles as teacher educators.

Requirements for teacher educators are changing. There is an increasing expectation that we publish more scholarly articles, preferably in refereed national journals. This is very much in contrast to the old "teach and serve" model under which many of us were initially hired. Conducting research and publishing articles are both very time consuming activities and some teacher educators fear that they will occur only at the expense of teaching excellence. This research and publication requirement presents newly hired faculty with a considerably more rigorous path to tenure and promotion than faculty members faced a decade or more ago.

How I Became A Teacher Educator

Henry V. Moyana
Zimbabwe

Early Education

I grew up in what was then Southern Rhodesia now known as Zimbabwe. It was in Southern Rhodesia that I went to primary or elementary school. After elementary school, I went on to junior school which I completed in 1957. Junior school students sit an examination known as the Form II examination. This is the equivalent of the second year of secondary school. When I completed my Form II examination, because there were several younger brothers and sisters behind me, it was decided that I go for a teacher training course which lasted two years. This would enable me to work as a teacher and so help my family educate the rest of the children.

I went to a teachers college called Umtali Teachers College starting in January 1958. I completed the course in December 1959. It was at that college that I developed interest in teacher education. The man who taught us teaching methods and practicals was an Irish man called Mr. Warke. Mr. Warke was a man of exceptional ability in the field of teaching. He could handle a class of Grade 1 children so well that he maintained their interest right through the lesson. The students admired his skills and wished they could one day acquire the same skills.

Teaching Experience

I started teaching at a place called Mt. Silinda Mission in 1960. Needless to say that Southern Rhodesia was a colonial society. Schools were segregated on racial

157

lines, European school supervisors were bossy and arrogant and school teachers and other African professionals felt trampled and humiliated. Teaching in the primary school was particularly frustrating. All teachers in the primary schools did not possess degree qualifications. Consequently they were not listened to by the authorities even when they had a good point of view. Although Mt. Silinda Mission was run by American missionaries, government school inspectors periodically harassed the teachers. Then, some of the missionaries themselves were quite racist and complemented the ruling colonial regime in certain ways.

Having observed these problems during the course of my teaching in the primary school, I resolved to go forward with my education. I decided to study for the high school certificate commonly known as 'O' level in this country. I did this privately by correspondence as I was teaching full time. I did not register with any school. I simply registered for the examination and read the relevant books. I did this in 1963 and passed all the five subjects in one year with a distinction in history. Once I got the high school certificate the road to degree work was now open. I then went to the University of Rhodesia in 1965 to do 'A' Level which is a preparatory course for university work. The course lasted one year. When I completed the course, the American missionaries offered me a scholarship to Defiance College in Ohio, U.SsA.

University Experience

I left for Defiance in 1967. I enrolled there in the fall of that year, but transferred to Columbia University a year later. I majored in history and English literature. When I completed my degree in 1971, I returned home and taught at a secondary school until September. I again returned to Columbia for graduate school. I now specialised in African and Pan African history. I completed my master's degree in 1972 and went straight into the doctoral programme. In May 1975 I graduated at Columbia earning two more degrees, the Master of Philosophy and the doctoral degree. My thesis was on 'Land Apportionment in Southern Rhodesia 1890-1970.'

By the time I completed my doctoral degree I had taught at the State University of New York at New Paltz and was now teaching at Lincoln University in Pennsylvania. I started at Lincoln University in 1973. Teaching African and Pan African history at Lincoln was one of the best experiences in my teaching career. I became Head of the History Department after teaching there for only one year. It was a rewarding experience.

Teacher Education

While I was in the U.S.A., the war of national liberation in Rhodesia assumed new levels of intensity. The news reaching us in America was patchy but encouraging. It became increasingly difficult to work in America while the war progressed in Rhodesia. I felt like playing a part in this process of decolonisation. I was a scholar and was best suited to decolonise the mind. Armed with African history and Pan African history, I felt I had the suitable tools necessary for the process of decolonising the mind. The danger in any colonial situation is that once the colonial flag has come down and independence proclaimed, the mind could remain colonised for centuries. The colonisation of the mind is one of colonialism's worst vices. British and French subjects in many parts of Africa still think British or French thirty years after independence. This is the area in which I thought of playing a role.

I originally intended to go to Rhodesia on sabbatical for a year. Lincoln University granted me the sabbatical for a year. I applied to the Ministry of Education for a teaching vacancy. They offered both my wife and I teaching posts at a teachers' college called Mkoba. The Ministry was anxious to make friends with educated Africans now that African nationalism was knocking at their doorsteps. But in this case they miscalculated. We took up our teaching posts in January 1977. I became head of the History Department and was charged with the responsibility of formulating a syllabus. I did it with zeal. History in our schools had always been taught from a Eurocentric point of view. The Napoleons and William of Normandys had always been hailed as the heroes of history. King Chaka, the mighty Zulu, Queen Nzinga of Angola and other African heroes such as Lobengula who resisted the imposition of colonialism had always been depicted as obstructors to European 'civilising mission.' Now, I had the chance to alter all that at the stroke of a pen. But even better, I could now teach the new history myself.

In the syllabus, I included such authors and activists as Walter Rodney, W. E. Du Bois, Marcus Garvey, Edward Wilmon Blyden, Malcolm X and many others. All these were anathema to the colonial regime. After the writing of the syllabus, we were to send it to the local university which was mainly staffed by colonial reactionaries for approval. When they received the syllabus they were so alarmed that they took it to the Ministry of Education where they argued that the Ministry had hired a revolutionary. Before too long I was summoned to appear before my principal who simply told me that my syllabus was unacceptable to the University and to the Ministry. I argued back citing academic freedom as an indispensable principle in syllabus formulation. In the end I refused to amend the syllabus and returned it to the university as it was. I was encouraged to transfer to another college where there was an established syllabus. In 1978 I transferred to Umtali Teachers College where I had studied earlier. As soon as I got there I again made amendments to the syllabus. By then independence was just around the corner and victory was certainly on my side. I had postponed my return to Lincoln at the end of 1977 and at the end of 1978. I informed Lincoln University that the struggle in Rhodesia was too hot to leave behind and that they should go ahead and hire somebody else.

Independence came in 1980 and Southern Rhodesia became Zimbabwe. In 1981 the new government promoted me to the position of Vice Principal. In 1983 I was promoted to the position of Principal of a teachers' college, a position which I held until I moved to Head Office in 1989. I am now the Executive Secretary for the National Council for Higher Education which grants accreditation to new universities and advises Government on all issues relating to higher education. I still deal with teachers' colleges on a policy formulation level.

Narratives by the Editors

As editors, we are including our narratives in this book because we felt we should share with you our "story" of how we became teacher educators. Our paths are quite similar to the paths of many of our colleagues. We began as teachers in the public schools. While in graduate programs we were involved in teaching and supervising students in teacher preparation programs. After receiving our doctorates, we both pursued careers as college and university professors in departments and schools of education. Thus we became teacher educators.

TEACHER EDUCATION: A FULFILLING CAREER

George A. Churukian
United States of America

Teacher education is not a career option most children are familiar with, and, as a child, I was no exception. I did not plan on becoming a teacher educator, but that is where my career path led me. Over the years, many factors influenced my career, and although I am now retired from full-time employment, I remain committed to teacher education.

One factor that led me to teacher education was my own education. Although I was born in Cleveland, Ohio in 1932, by the time I was eight years old, my family and I were living in the much smaller community of Paris, Illinois. I attended Millikin University in Decatur, Illinois where I received, in 1955, an undergraduate degree [Bachelor of Science (B.S.)] in biology-chemistry. After earning my degree, I obtained a position as a quality control chemist for a company that made adhesives, but left that job in the fall of 1955 to attend graduate school to study psychology. After a year of graduate study, I returned to industry as a supervisor at a chemical company for a year before reentering graduate school.

My purpose for returning to graduate school was to become certified to teach science in the public schools. I found the coursework I needed at the University of Illinois. Upon completion of the certification, my teaching career began in September 1958 as a teacher of seventh grade (12 year old students) science. I taught at the junior high school level for eight years. During my last three years of teaching

163

at the junior high school level, I was the building representative for the science department. In addition to my teaching responsibilities of five classes, I was responsible for coordinating the curriculum of the department, overseeing the budget, and supervising the nine member science faculty. While I was teaching, I attended Hofstra University in a secondary education master's program, receiving my degree [Master of Science (M.S.)] in 1963.

Although I enjoyed teaching and being building representative of the science department, I was interested in accepting more responsibilities, and when the position of science department chair became open, I applied. In addition to teaching, the position of department chair included coordinating the science program throughout the school district from grades K through 12. I did not receive the appointment because I did not have the necessary course work in the area of supervision and curriculum. In order to obtain proper credentials, I applied and was accepted into the doctoral program at Syracuse University in the fall of 1966.

While at Syracuse University, I was granted a graduate assistantship with the Urban Teacher Preparation Program. This program was established in 1964 as a master's program to prepare individuals to become teachers in inner city schools. During the five years that I was associated with the program, I went from being a graduate assistant to assistant professor and associate director for instruction of the program, having received my doctorate [Doctor of Philosophy (Ph.D.)] in June 1970.

When I began my studies at Syracuse, my intent was to return to teaching in the public schools as a department chair or curriculum coordinator. However, my graduate assistantship with the Urban Teacher Preparation Program provided me the opportunity to become a teacher educator.

I left Syracuse in the fall of 1971 to take the position of Director of Teacher Education at Virginia Wesleyan College in Norfolk, Virginia. Virginia Wesleyan was a new institution, having been founded just five years before. It was a good place to begin my career in teacher education because my major responsibilities were varied. Not only did I develop the education curriculum, I also taught, supervised, and advised future teachers.

My career path led me back to Illinois when, in 1976, I left Virginia Wesleyan to take a similar position at Illinois Wesleyan University in Bloomington, Illinois. Along with its "twin" city of Normal, Bloomington has a metropolitan population of about 100,000.

Illinois Wesleyan University, a liberal arts institution founded in 1850, is comprised of the College of Liberal Arts; the College of Fine Arts made up of the Schools of Art, Music, and Theater Arts; and the School of Nursing. With approximately 1,850 students, IWU supports 145 full-time faculty and a number of adjunct faculty members. The education department houses about 180 students preparing to become teachers in elementary education; in the secondary education areas of biology, chemistry, physics, history, mathematics, English, French, and Spanish; and in music education. The university only offers undergraduate degrees, having no graduate programs.

My responsibilities at Illinois Wesleyan were many. As Director of Teacher Education and Chair of the Education Department, I taught educational psychology, secondary curriculum and instructional procedures, and conducted the secondary student teacher seminar. I also supervised student teachers, supervised secondary pre-student teachers, and coordinated and evaluated all teacher education programs. In addition, I interviewed and advised all students entering the teacher education program, and placed all student teachers for their student teaching experience. Besides working with students, I was responsible for the departmental budget; designing, writing, editing, and submitting the state self study reports in preparation for state visitations to re-accredit the teacher education programs; and acting as liaison with the local school districts and Illinois Board of Education. I developed the teacher education curriculum, coordinated the supervision of university supervisors, and worked with public school personnel. I was also active in the state and national teacher education associations, serving on committees at both the state and national level, and holding office (including president) at the state level.

Most of my teaching responsibilities were with students preparing to teach at the secondary level. My major objectives were to provide the students with the basic theories of human development, learning, and instruction; to help them learn the skills necessary to become effective teachers; to sensitize them to young students; and to provide field experiences in the schools of at least one hundred hours prior to student teaching. As a part of the teaching process, I advised students on whether or not they should continue in the field of teaching.

My responsibilities as a teacher educator were not unusual. Teacher educators are expected to teach, supervise student teachers, advise, serve on university committees, do research, write and present papers at learned associations, publish in referred journals, maintain relationships with the public schools and state education department, and be of service to the community. Illinois Wesleyan expected me to use my professional time in the approximate percentages: 60% teaching, 5% student advising and committee work, 20% administrating the department and teacher education programs, 10% research, and 5% service to the community. In reality, my time was spent quite differently. I spent 40% of my time teaching, 20% advising and committee work, 40% administrating, and I felt fortunate I could squeeze in any time for research and community service.

One of the highlights of my career as a teacher educator was as a Fulbright Scholar. I spent five months, January through June 1992, as a consultant to the Faculty of the School of Education at Kuwait University, Kuwait. This was one year after the end of the Gulf War. The schools had only been in session for a semester. The people of Kuwait were working very hard to heal the many wounds and to rebuild what was destroyed. The experience was rewarding and exciting, one which I will never forget.

I retired as a full time faculty member in August of 1993 after completing 35 years as a teacher and teacher educator. However, I remain active and committed to teacher education by teaching a course or two each year.

I also remain interested in the issues facing teachers and teacher educators today. One of the most serious problems in schools today is violence. Students tend to react in a violent manner when confronted with someone or something that upsets them. They may not have learned that there are other ways to settle problems. Teachers and school administrators often have a difficult time dealing with these problems since our society has become confrontational. What is happening in the schools is a reflection of society. To combat this situation would take a concerted effort by teachers, administrators, parents, school boards, local governments, religious groups, and students working toward a common goal of a safe and caring environment both inside and outside of school.

Teacher education needs to change to become more people oriented rather than process oriented. We need to add more of the affective domain to our curriculum along with the current emphasis on the cognitive domain. I see little movement in this direction, even though research over the past 40 years have indicated that creating a caring school environment does have beneficial results. We need to prepare teacher educators who are sensitive to others.

166

This caring for and sensitivity to others is what led me into teacher education. Although my career path seems circuitous at first, the many experiences I gathered along the way contributed to my success as a teacher educator. I have seen former students become teachers and leaders in their own right and am glad that I could contribute toward their careers. Teacher education has been a rewarding and fulfilling career for me.

A Personal Journey to Teacher Education

Corey R. Lock
United States of America

As an eighteen year old college student in 1961, I decided to become an English major. I loved reading and the English classes were very enjoyable. I learned to analyze and interpret poetry. In addition I became involved with theatre and drama, and I had many opportunities to write. But, most importantly, I was introduced to the classics. I read and studied, and before I realized it, I had taken almost half of all my college classes in English and English related coursework. Unfortunately, there were not many career choices for an English major.

During my junior year the University began posting notices around the campus that described the need for teachers in the public schools. There was even loan money available for students who studied to become schoolteachers. So I made an appointment with the teacher education faculty to see what the requirements were to become a teacher. I received a list of classes to take that would lead to teacher certification.

As I progressed through the teacher education program I was still not certain that I wanted to teach. But the coursework was interesting and during student teaching I discovered that working with adolescents was really enjoyable. So, I decided to become a high school English teacher.

After completing my bachelor's degree and receiving my teacher's certificate, I accepted a position as a teacher of English to fifteen-year-olds in a high school of about 1,500 students. I was assigned to teach the same subject five periods a day. Each period was fifty-five minutes, so I repeated the same lessons five times each day.

It didn't take long for me to discover that what I thought teachers did and what students thought teachers did were two different things. I wanted to help students learn about the power and beauty of good writing, but students wanted to do anything but learn about the power and beauty of good writing. Just about everything I learned in my teacher education program did not prepare me for the challenges students gave me that first year. Sometimes I felt as if I had been catapulted into the "real" world of teaching where there were unmotivated students, uninvolved parents, insensitive administrators, an uninspired curriculum, and a system that obstructed creativity at every turn. And, I didn't have a clue how to alter the situation.

The summer after my first year of teaching I did a lot of soul-searching about how I thought a classroom should function and what I needed to do to make my classroom function successfully. During this same summer I enrolled in a university graduate program for teachers. I learned that there were solutions for many of the problems I had encountered and I couldn't wait for the school year to begin so I could try out these techniques. Consequently, I spent the next several years identifying solutions for difficult classroom problems. By the beginning of my fourth year of teaching I was appointed chair of the English department. In addition to teaching, professional responsibilities included helping new teachers resolve instructional problems, and creating professional development experiences for a staff of eighteen English teachers.

By that time I was completing my master's degree and my advisor was encouraging me to apply for a Ph.D. program in curriculum and instruction. In the meantime, my advisor arranged for me to begin teaching college classes for prospective teachers. By using the material on teacher problems that I had been collecting for years, I was able to give prospective teachers what I thought was a realistic view of the classroom. This experience convinced me that I wanted to work in a teacher education program and that my contribution to education would come through preparing my students to acquire more effective teaching skills.

There are only a few programs that prepare people to become teacher educators. I enrolled in the doctoral program in Curriculum and Instruction at The Ohio State University which offered a series of classes on the topic of teacher education. While in the doctoral program I taught one day a week in the schools to stay current with teacher practices. And, I decided to write a dissertation on a teacher education topic.

My first university teaching position was at Marshall University, a school with a good reputation for preparing classroom teachers. I taught classes in educational foundations, methods of teaching in high school, and I supervised student teachers. It was at Marshall that I discovered two very real problems in teacher education. First, there was a perception among many that the experiences students received in teacher education programs were not very useful when it came to actual practice. I had experienced this problem in my own preparation program. Second, there were many students who believed they already knew how to teach without any training. These two problems came to dominate the redesign of Marshall's teacher education program. Through this process I gained some insights working with my colleagues. After I had been at Marshall for about ten years I was appointed to direct the teacher education program. During this time I discovered the importance of teacher educators establishing and maintaining credibility by developing close relationships with the schools.

A few years later I moved to the University of North Carolina at Charlotte as chair of the Department of Curriculum and Instruction. This was a much larger program than the one at Marshall. The Faculty of Education's first job was to prepare for a national accreditation of our teacher education program. I was the point person, the individual selected to coordinate the accreditation process. We had to document a knowledge base for our program, sequence the classes, and develop admissions criteria for entry into teacher education. This was interesting work because the entire teacher education faculty had to work together and agree on how to prepare students to become teachers. It was this experience that allowed me to see the power of a teacher education program versus a series of loosely related classes.

In recent years my work in teacher education has moved out of the university and into the public schools. While most of our classes require students to spend large amounts of time observing and working with teachers, I moved my classes to an actual high school setting in a local high school. My class is able to go directly from my classroom to a high school classroom. I am able to bring school personnel to my classroom to talk about how to be a successful teacher. My students now leave the classroom and enter the halls of the public school. They see and hear students talking, interacting, and socializing. My students see the school in operation on a daily basis rather than hearing about high schools in the abstract while sitting in a college class. I believe this is a more realistic approach to preparing students to become high school teachers.

In 1988 I became interested in teacher education in other countries. Through groups like the International Society for Teacher Education (ISTE) and the International Council on Education for Teaching (ICET), I have been able to learn how teacher educators in other countries prepared students to become teachers. This is a fascinating area of study. I have focused on trying to determine if there is a body of knowledge that is common to teacher educators in countries throughout the world.

I think the new challenge for teacher educators is to find new and innovative ways to assist practicing teachers in the field. Some of the things we are beginning to do are delivering classes on site, using the school's schedule rather than the university's to schedule classes, using Saturday and evening time slots, and tailoring coursework around the issues of individual teachers and schools. Education in the United States is becoming more and more inclusive; consequently, teachers and schools want to develop new skills and techniques so they can effectively teach all the children who attend their schools.

MELLEN STUDIES IN EDUCATION

1. C. J. Schott, **Improving The Training and Evaluation of Teachers at the Secondary School Level: Educating the Educators in Pursuit of Excellence**

2. Manfred Prokop, **Learning Strategies For Second Language Users: An Analytical Appraisal with Case Studies**

3. Charles P. Nemeth, **A Status Report on Contemporary Criminal Justice Education: A Definition of the Discipline and an Assessment of Its Curricula, Faculty and Program Characteristics**

4. Stephen H. Barnes (ed.), **Points of View on American Higher Education: A Selection of Essays from** *The Chronicle of Higher Education* (Volume 1) **Professors and Scholarship**

5. Stephen H. Barnes (ed.), **Points of View on American Higher Education: A Selection of Essays from** *The Chronicle of Higher Education* (Volume 2) **Institutions and Issues**

6. Stephen H. Barnes (ed.), **Points of View on American Higher Education: A Selection of Essays from** *The Chronicle of Higher Education* (Volume 3) **Students and Standards**

7. Michael V. Belok and Thomas Metos, **The University President in Arizona 1945-1980: An Oral History**

8. Henry R. Weinstock and Charles J. Fazzaro, **Democratic Ideals and the Valuing of Knowledge In American Education: Two Contradictory Tendencies**

9. Arthur R. Crowell, Jr., **A Handbook For the Special Education Administrator: Organization and Procedures for Special Education**

10. J.J. Chambliss, **The Influence of Plato and Aristotle on John Dewey's Philosophy**

11. Alan H. Levy, **Elite Education and the Private School: Excellence and Arrogance at Phillips Exeter Academy**

12. James J. Van Patten (ed.), **Problems and Issues in College Teaching and Higher Education Leadership**

13. Célestin Freinet, **The Wisdom of Matthew: An Essay in Contemporary French Educational Theory**, John Sivell (trans.)